THE
MIRROR
MAKER

THE

MIRROR

MAKER

STORIES & ESSAYS
BY PRIMO LEVI

Translated from the Italian
by Raymond Rosenthal

858
L

SCHOCKEN BOOKS   NEW YORK

Levi, Primo.
[Racconti e saggi. English]
The mirror maker : stories and essays / by Primo Levi ; translated
from the Italian by Raymond Rosenthal.
p.   cm.
Translation of: Racconti e saggi.
ISBN 0-8052-4076-4
1. Levi, Primo—Translations, English.   I. Title.
PQ4872.E8R313   1989
853'.914—dc20   89-42680

Manufactured in the United States of America
Book Design by Fearn Cutler
First American Edition

CONTENTS

. . .

ESSAYS

PREFACE
PRIMO LEVI'S MUSE: CURIOSITY

■ ■ ■

Primo Levi does not like to write articles on the spur of the moment; the first emotion aroused in him by a piece of news or an event must be left to be decanted, to pass through the filter of reflection. Thus, in this collection, which documents more than twenty years of his collaboration with *La Stampa*, the articles for particular occasions are few, and in any case they are dictated by a compelling concern that guarantees their freshness. As the critic Massimo Mila used to say, there is never anything gratuitous or sterile in what Primo Levi writes.

The book we present here offers the full gamut of his human and expressive interests. There is the experience of the *Lager*, which at a distance of so many years acts as subdued cautery, the cautery of injured memory. One mustn't be deceived by certain ironic, marginal evocations: precisely in one of these "pieces" that seems to assume a tone of levity, he again speaks of the "drowned and saved," as he did in one of the chapters of *Survival in Auschwitz*,* his first book; but above all this anticipates the title of Levi's last, most profound probe, which by its stoical speculation about ethical evil goes beyond the very events of Nazism and its exemplary massacres. Words and themes surface on the page with a sense of irreducibility and have a great seminal power. Of course, this collection had to embody the passion of the man of science, in particular the chemist, eager to annex new continents for the territory of literature. And also the felicitousness of interchanges and graftings that are natural to the well-seasoned writer who is intolerant of specialized, sectorial limitations (the witness of the concentration camps, the "poet" of chemistry . . .).

What, then, am I saying? That in looking at Primo Levi the discourse on the two cultures, which seems remote and yet every so often reappears with different nuances and more up-to-date oppositions, loses its meaning and makes you wonder. For here we have the example of a writer who, without pretensions and without timidities, takes what is good for him where he finds it, practicing an ideal of unitary culture, where forking paths do not exist. To be convinced of this, one only has to read the praise he bestows on poetry, to which he thinks all of us are genetically predisposed, and his salutary "violence" against the "violations" of current language.

What a lesson for the narcissism of the literati and the boastfulness of the technophiles! In reality Primo Levi remains faithful to the motto of the ancient poet: *"Homo sum: humani nihil a me alienum puto"*—"I'm a man and I believe that nothing human is alien to me." It is an attitude of solidarity, through good and evil, with the human species. But

---

* Translation of Levi's *Se questo è un uomo*; published in England as *If This Is a Man.* —TRANS.

among the virtues of his fellow men Primo Levi has a predilection for the will to experiment and to understand. His truest muse, the one that inspires and links together pages apparently so far apart, is curiosity. Curiosity is the "cheerful strength" that, no matter how weakened and humiliated, compels the writer to spy out in the *Lager* the monstrous logic of annihilation; the very same logic that leads him to envy the astronauts in their flight to the stars. He confesses and justifies these divigations with a naturalness that enchants: "I've always strived to pass from the darkness into the light . . ."

Lorenzo Mondo

THE
MIRROR
MAKER

P R E M I S E
...

I hope that the reader will be indulgent toward the extreme dispersion of themes, tones, and angles of approach that he will find in this collection. My justification is: the "pieces" are situated in an arc of time that is close to a quarter of a century, the time of my almost total fidelity to *La Stampa*: and in twenty-five years many things change, inside us and around us. Furthermore, they are conditioned by my intrinsic libertinage, in part willed, in part due to the itinerary fate has reserved for me; I've drunk at various founts and breathed different airs, some salutary, others quite polluted. I'm neither sorry for this nor do I complain: "the world is beautiful because it is varied," quotes the protagonist of one of my books, with his typical lack of originality.

I beg the reader not to go in search of messages. It is a term that I detest because it distresses me greatly, for it forces on me clothes that are not mine, which in fact belong to a human type that I distrust: the prophet, the soothsayer, the seer. I am none of these; I'm a normal man with a good memory who fell into a maelstrom and got out of it more by luck than by virtue, and who from that time on has preserved a certain curiosity about maelstroms large and small, metaphorical and actual.

Primo Levi
October 1986

TO MY FRIENDS
. . .

Dear friends, I say friends here
In the larger sense of the word:
Wife, sister, associates, relatives,
Schoolmates, men and women,
Persons seen only once
Or frequented all my life:
Provided that between us, for at least a moment,
Was drawn a segment,
A well-defined chord.

I speak for you, companions on a journey
Dense, not devoid of effort,
And also for you who have lost
The soul, the spirit, the wish to live.
Or nobody or somebody, or perhaps only one, or you
Who are reading me: remember the time
Before the wax hardened,
When each of us was like a seal.
Each of us carries the imprint
Of the friend met along the way;
In each the trace of each.

For good or evil
In wisdom or in folly
Each stamped by each.

Now that time presses urgently,
And the tasks are finished,
To all of you the modest wish
That the autumn may be long and mild.

S T O R I E S

T H E   T H A W

. . .

When the snow will all have melted
We shall search for the old path,
The one that is being covered by brambles
Behind the monastery's walls;
Everything will be as it once was.

On either side, amid the thick heather
We shall again find certain frail herbs
Whose name I would not know how to say:
I read up on it every Friday,
But every Saturday it leaves my mind:
I've been told that they are rare
And good for curing melancholy.

The ferns bordering the road
Are like tender creatures:
They barely push up from the ground,
Curled in a spiral, and yet
Right now they are ready for their loves
Alternate and green, more intricate than ours.

Their germs chafe at the bit,
Tiny males and tiny females,
In the rusty sporangium.
They will erupt at the first rain,
Swimming in the first drop,
Eager and agile: long live the bride and groom!

We are tired of winter. The bite
Of frost has left its mark
On flesh, minds, mud, and wood.
Let the thaw come and melt the memory
Of last year's snow.

T H E   I N T E R V I E W

▪ ▪ ▪

It was still pitch-dark, and it was drizzling. Elio was coming
home from the night shift, and he was tired and sleepy; he
got off the streetcar and walked toward home, first by a
street with an uneven roadbed, then along a small alley that
was not lit. In the darkness he heard a voice that asked him,
"Would you agree to an interview?" It was a slightly metallic
voice, devoid of dialectal inflection; strangely, it seemed to
him that it was coming from below, close to his feet. He
stopped, a bit surprised, and answered yes, but that he was
in a hurry to get home.

"I'm in a hurry too, don't worry," the voice answered.
"It won't take two minutes. Tell me: how many inhabitants
are there on the earth?"

"More or less, four billion. But why are you asking me,
of all people?"

"Purely by chance, believe me. I did not have the opportunity to select. Listen, please: how do you digest?"

Elio was annoyed. "What do you mean, how do you
digest? Some digest well, some don't. Who are you, anyway?

I hope you're not trying to sell me some medicine at this hour, and here in the dark in the middle of the street?"

"No, I'm just collecting statistics," the voice said, unperturbed. "I come from a nearby star, we are supposed to compile an annual directory of the galaxies' inhabited planets, and we need some comparative data."

"And . . . how is it that you speak such good Italian?"

"I also speak several other languages. You know, your TV transmissions do not stop at the ionosphere but continue into space. They take a good eleven years, but they reach us quite distinctly. That, for example, is how I learned your language. I find your commercial vignettes interesting: they are very instructive, and I believe I've understood how you eat and what you eat, but none of us has an idea of how you digest. Therefore, I must ask you to please answer my question."

"Well, you know, I've always digested well and I couldn't give you many details. We have a . . . a sack that is called the stomach, with acids inside, and then a tube. You eat, two or three hours go by, and the food dissolves; in short, it becomes flesh and blood."

". . . flesh and blood," the voice repeated, as though taking notes. Elio noticed that the voice was precisely like those heard on TV: clear but insipid and lifeless.

"Why do you spend so much time washing yourselves and washing the objects around you?"

Elio, with a certain embarrassment, explained that one washes only for a few minutes each day, that one washes so as not to be dirty, and that if one stays dirty there is the danger of catching some disease.

"Right, that was one of our hypotheses. You wash in order not to die. How do you die? At what age? Does everybody die?"

Here too Elio's answer was a bit confused. He said that

there weren't any rules, both young and old died, very few got to be a hundred. "I understand. Those who use white sheets and wash their floors live long." Elio tried to rectify this, but the interviewer was in a hurry and continued, "How do you reproduce?"

More and more embarrassed, Elio got entangled in a complicated disquisition concerning man and woman, on chromosomes (about which in fact he'd been informed a few days earlier by the TV), on heredity, gestation, and parturition, but the stranger interrupted him: he wanted to know at what age clothes begin to develop. While by now out of patience, Elio was explaining that clothes don't grow on the person but are bought, he noticed that dawn was breaking, and in the uncertain light he saw that the voice issued from a sort of puddle at his feet; or rather, not exactly a puddle but something like a big splotch of brown marmalade.

The stranger must also have realized that quite a lot of time had passed. The voice said, "Thanks a lot, forgive the imposition." Immediately after that the splotch contracted and stretched upward, as though trying to detach itself from the ground. It seemed to Elio that it couldn't succeed, and the voice could still be heard saying, "Please, could you be so kind as to light a match? Sometimes if I'm not surrounded by a bit of ionized air I'm unable to take off." Elio lit a match, and as if sucked up by a vacuum cleaner the splotch rose and vanished into the smoky morning sky.

May 22, 1977

THEY WERE MADE TO BE TOGETHER

...

It was the first time that Plato was able to arrange a real date with a girl. Plato lived with his family in a small, single-family house, charming but rather small: everything was very simple, so much so that the front door was only a thin brown rectangle turning upon a point. The girl was called Surpha and lived not far away: we mean to say not far away as the crow flies, because between the two dwellings ran a brook, and Plato could only traverse the distance by coasting along the brook and going around its source, which was, however, approximately thirty kilometers away, or by wading or swimming (for him it was all the same).

There were no bridges, because in that place there was neither above nor below, and therefore a bridge could not exist, nor even be imagined; for the same reason, it was not imaginable to cross the brook by straddling or leaping over it, even though it was not very wide. In short, according to our usual criteria, it was an uncomfortable country: there was no way to cross or negotiate the brook without getting wet, so Plato swam to the other side, and then he dried off by turning in the sun, which slowly ran along the horizon.

Since he planned to arrive before night, he resumed walking at a good clip without letting himself be distracted by the landscape, which in reality did not offer much: a circular line around him, interrupted here and there by the green segments of trees, behind which appeared and disappeared the intensely luminous segment of the sun.

After an hour's walk Plato begin to distinguish, to the left of the sun, the small green-blue dash of Surpha's house: he soon reached it and was glad to see the girl coming to meet him, a slim small line which, however, kept growing longer as the distance diminished; soon he distinguished the red and yellow dashes of her favorite skirt, and soon afterward the two held out their hands. They did not grasp them: they were content to wedge one hand inside the other by splaying their fingers, but they both experienced a slight shiver of pleasure.

They conversed at length, looking into each other's eyes, even though this forced them into an unnatural cramped position; the hours went by and their desire grew. The sun was dying: Surpha found a way to let Plato know that there was no one at home and no one would come back until late at night.

Timid and irresolute, Plato entered that sweet house, which he did not yet know, even though he had visited it innumerable times in his dreams. They did not light the lamp: they withdrew to the most sheltered corner, and while they were still talking, Plato felt his profile deliciously assume a new outline, so much so that one of its sides reproduced in the negative, with great precision, the girl's corresponding side: they were made for one another.

At last they joined, in the darkness and in the solemn silence of the plain, and they were a single figure, delimited by a single contour; and in that magic instant, but only with an immediately vanished flash, through both flared the intuition of a different world, infinitely more rich and complex, in which the prison of the horizon was broken, annulled by a refulgent concave sky, and in which their bodies, shadows without thickness, instead blossomed out new, solid and full. But the vision surpassed their intention and lasted but an instant. They separated and bade each other goodbye, and Plato sadly started on his way home, gliding along the now dark plain.

November 27, 1977

THE GREAT MUTATION
■ ■ ■

For several days now Isabella had been restless: she ate little, had a slight fever, and complained about an itch on her back. Her family was busy running the store and did not have much time to devote to her: "She's probably developing," her mother said; she kept her on a diet and gave her massages with a salve, but the itch increased. The girl was no longer able to sleep; as she applied the salve, her mother noticed that the skin was rough: it was beginning to be covered with hairs, thick, stiff, short, and whitish. At that she got frightened, consulted with the father, and they sent for the doctor.

The doctor examined her. He was young and charming, and Isabella noticed with astonishment that at the beginning of the examination he appeared preoccupied and perplexed, then increasingly attentive and interested, and in the end he seemed as happy as though he had won the lottery. He announced that it wasn't anything serious, but that he had to review certain books of his and would come back the next day.

The next day, he returned with a magnifying glass and showed to her father and mother that those hairs were ramified and flat: in fact, they weren't hairs but rather feathers that were growing. He was even more cheerful than the day before.

"Buck up, Isabella," he said. "There's nothing to be afraid of. In four months you'll be able to fly."

Then, turning to the parents, he added a rather confused explanation. Was it possible that they did not know anything? Didn't they read the newspapers? Didn't they watch television? "It's a case of Major Mutation, the first in Italy, and it's actually in our parts, in this forgotten valley!" The wings would form little by little, without damage to the organism, and then there would probably be other cases in the neighborhood, perhaps among the girl's schoolmates, because this thing was contagious.

"But if it's contagious, it's an illness!" the father said.

"It is contagious, apparently it's a virus, but it's not an illness. Why should all viral infections be harmful? Flying is a beautiful thing; I would like it myself, if only to visit the patients in the outlying hamlets. This is the first case in Italy, as I already told you, and I'll report it to the provincial physician's office, but the phenomenon has already been described: several centers of infection have already been observed in Canada, Sweden, and Japan. But just think, what a piece of luck for you and for me!"

That it actually was a piece of luck Isabella wasn't all that convinced. The feathers were growing rapidly: they bothered her when she lay in bed, and you could see them through her blouse. Along about March the new bone structure was already quite visible, and by the end of May the separation of the wings from her back was almost complete.

Then came photographers, journalists, Italian and foreign medical committees: Isabella enjoyed herself and felt important, but she answered all questions seriously and with dignity, and in any case the questions were stupid and always the same. She did not dare discuss it with her parents, since she did not want to frighten them, but she was alarmed: very well, she would have wings, but where would she learn to fly? At the driving school in the provincial capital? Or the Poggio Merli airport? She would have liked to have the public-health doctor teach her: or what if he too sprouted wings, hadn't he said that they were contagious? So they would have gone together to see patients in the hamlets; and perhaps they would even have passed beyond the mountains and flown together over the sea, side by side, beating their wings in the same cadence.

■ ■ ■

In June, at the end of the school year, Isabella's wings were well formed and very beautiful to look at. They matched the color of her hair (Isabella was blond): on top toward the shoulders they were sprinkled with golden-brown dots, but the tips were snow-white, shiny, and robust. A commission came from the National Research Council, a substantial grant came from UNICEF, and there also came a physiotherapist from Sweden: she stayed at the only inn in the village, didn't understand Italian very well, nothing suited her, and she got Isabella to do a series of very boring exercises.

Boring and useless: Isabella felt her new muscles quiver and stretch, she watched the sure flight of the swallows in the summer sky, she no longer had any doubts, and she had the definite sensation that she would be able to learn to fly by herself, that indeed she already knew how to fly: by now at night she dreamt of nothing else. The Swede was strict, she had made it clear to her that she must wait some more, that she mustn't expose herself to dangers, but Isabella was only waiting for the opportunity to present itself to her. When she was able to be by herself on a sloping meadow, or sometimes even in her closed room, she tried to beat her wings; she heard their harsh rustle in the air, and in her small adolescent shoulders she felt a strength that almost frightened her. The gravity of her body had become hateful to her; when she fanned her wings, she felt it reduce her body weight, almost annul it—almost. The call of the earth was still too strong, a halter, a chain.

The opportunity arrived about the middle of August. The Swede, on vacation, had returned to her country, and Isabella's parents were at the store, busy with the summer visitors. Isabella took the Costalunga mule path, went past the ridge, and reached the steep meadows on the opposite slope: nobody was there. She crossed herself, as when you dive into the water, opened her wings, and began to run down the hill. At each step the impact with the ground became lighter until the earth vanished under her feet; she felt a great peace, and the air whistled in her ears. She stretched her legs out behind her: she regretted not having put on jeans, her skirt fluttered in the wind and got in her way.

Her arms and hands also got in her way, she tried to cross them over her chest, then she held them stiffly along her sides. Who ever said that flying was difficult? There was nothing easier in the world, she wanted to laugh and sing. If she increased the slant of the wings, her flight slowed down and pointed upward, but only briefly; then her speed fell off too much, and Isabella felt in danger. She tried beating her wings, and she felt supported, gaining height with each beat, easily, without effort.

Also, changing direction was as easy as a game, you learned how immediately, all you had to do was give a slight twist to the right wing and you immediately turned to the right. You didn't even have to think about it, the wings themselves thought of it, just as the feet think of making you turn right or left when you walk. Suddenly she sensed a swelling, a tension in her lower abdomen; she felt damp, she touched it, and her hand came away smeared with blood. But she knew what it was, she knew that one day or another it would happen, and she wasn't frightened.

...

She stayed in the air for a good hour and learned that from the Gravio's boulders rose a current of warm air that helped her gain altitude without effort. She followed the provincial highway and hovered right above the village, at a height of perhaps two hundred meters: she saw a passerby stop, then point at the sky for another passerby; the second looked up, then he ran to the store, and out of it came her mother and her father with two or three customers. Soon the streets swarmed with people. She would have liked to land in the piazza, but in fact there were too many people and she was afraid of landing badly and being laughed at.

She let the wind carry her beyond the stream, over the meadows behind the mill. She descended, continued to descend until she could distinguish the clover's pink flowers. Also, when it came to landing it seemed the wings knew better than she did: it seemed to them natural to be set vertically and churn violently as though to fly backwards; she lowered her legs and found herself standing on the grass, just the slightest bit out of breath. She folded her wings and set out for home.

In the autumn four of Isabella's schoolmates sprouted wings, three boys and a girl; on Sunday mornings it was amusing to see them chase each other in midair around the church's bell tower. In December the mailman's son got wings, and he immediately replaced his father, to everyone's great advantage. The doctor grew wings the next year, but he no longer took an interest in Isabella, and in great haste he married a young woman without wings who came from the city.

Isabella's father sprouted wings when he was already over fifty. He did not draw great profit from them: with fear and vertigo he took a few lessons from his daughter, and he twisted an ankle in landing. The wings wouldn't let him sleep, they filled his bed with feathers and down, and he found it difficult to put on his shirt, jacket, and coat. They also were a hindrance when he was behind the counter in the store, and so he had them amputated.

August 21, 1983

THE TWO FLAGS
...

Bertrando was born and grew up in a country called Lantania that had a very beautiful flag: or at least that was how it seemed to Bertrando, to all of his friends and fellow students, and to the greater part of his compatriots. It was different from all the others: against a bright purple ground stood out an orange oval, and in this rose a volcano, green at the bottom and white with snow at its top, surmounted by a plume of smoke.

In Bertrando's country there were no volcanoes; but there was one in the bordering country, Gunduwia, with which Lantania had been for centuries at war, or at any rate in a hostile relationship. Indeed, the Lantanic national poem, in a passage of debatable interpretation, mentioned the volcano as the "Lantanic altar of fire."

In all of Lantania's schools it was taught that the annexation of the volcano by the Gunduwians had been an act of banditry, and that the first duty of every Lantanian was to train militarily, hate Gunduwia with all his might, and prepare for the inevitable and desirable war, which was going to bend Gunduwian arrogance and reconquer the volcano.

That this volcano every three or four years devastated thousands of villages and every year caused disastrous earthquakes was of no importance: Lantanic it was and Lantanic it must be again.

In any case, how not hate a country like Gunduwia? That very name, so grim, so sepulchral, inspired aversion. The Lantanians were a contentious and litigious people, they brawled or knifed each other for the slightest divergence of opinion, but they all agreed on the fact that Gunduwia was a country of scoundrels and bullies.

As for their flag, it represented them perfectly: it could not have been uglier, it was flat and silly, clumsy both in colors and design. Nothing more than a brown disk in a yellow field: not an image, not a symbol. A coarse, vulgar, and excremental flag. The Gunduwians must really be imbeciles, must have been since time immemorial for having chosen it and drenched it with their blood when they died in battle, something that happened three or four times a century. Furthermore, they were notoriously avaricious and wasteful, lewd and prudish, reckless and cowardly.

■ ■ ■

Bertrando was a proper young man, respectful of laws and traditions, and the very sight of his country's flag caused a wave of pride and self-assurance to course through his veins. The combination of those three noble colors, green, orange, and purple, when he sometimes recognized them joined in a spring meadow, made him strong and happy, glad to be a Lantanian, glad to be in this world, but also ready to die for his flag, best if wrapped in it.

Conversely, since his earliest childhood, since his memory began, the Gunduwian yellow and brown had been odious to him: disagreeable if taken separately, hateful to the point of nausea when placed side by side. Bertrando was a sensitive and emotional youth, and the sight of the enemy flag reproduced for derision on wall posters or in satirical vignettes put him in a bad mood and gave him an itch at the nape of the neck and elbows, intense salivation, and a certain dizziness.

Once, during a concert, he had found himself next to a pretty girl who inadvertently, of course, was wearing a yellow blouse and a brown skirt; Bertrando had been compelled to get up and move away and, since there were no other seats, to listen to the concert standing up; if he hadn't been rather shy, he would have told that girl exactly what she deserved. Bertrando liked apricots and medlars, but he ate them with his eyes shut so as to avoid the disgusting sight of the brown pit that stood out against the yellowish pulp.

Also, the sound of the Gunduwian language, which was harsh, guttural, almost inarticulate, had similar effects on Bertrando. It seemed to him scandalous that in certain Lantanian schools the enemy tongue should be taught, and that there even should be academicians who studied its history and origins, its grammar and syntax, and translated its literature. What sort of literature could that be? What good could come from that yellow-brown land of perverts and degenerates?

And yet there had been a professor who claimed he could prove that Lantanian and Gunduwian descended from one and the same language, extinct now for three thousand years, documented by a number of inscriptions on tombstones. Absurd, or rather insufferable. There are things that *cannot* be true, that must be ignored, not mentioned, buried. If it had been up to Bertrando, all Gunduwophiles would be buried three meters deep under the ground, along with all those (unfortunately, almost all of them young!) who, out of snobbism, surreptitiously listened to Gunduwian radio and repeated its obscene lies.

■ ■ ■

Not that the border between the two countries was hermetic. It was well patrolled on both sides by guards who shot readily, but there was a pass, and every so often trade delegations passed through it in both directions because the two economies were complementary. To everyone's surprise, there also passed through smugglers, with considerable loads that the border guards did not seem to notice.

Once Bertrando had watched a Gunduwian delegation pass through the main street of the capital. Those bastards were not really so different from the Lantanians: aside from their ridiculous way of dressing, they would have been difficult to pick out if not for their shifty eyes and their typically sly expressions. Bertrando had come closer, to sniff and find out whether it was true that they stank, but the police had prevented him. Of course, they had to stink. In the Lantanian subconscious there had been established for centuries an etymological nexus between Gunduwia and stench (*kumt* in Lantanian). Conversely, it was known to everyone that in Gunduwian *latnen* are boils, and to Lantanians this seemed a vicious buffoonery that must be washed in blood.

Now it so happened that, after long secret negotiations, the presidents of the two countries made it known that in the spring they would meet. After an embarrassed silence, the Lantanian daily newspaper began to leak unaccustomed material: photographs of the Gunduwian capital with its imposing cathedral and its beautiful parks; images of Gunduwian children, well groomed and with laughing eyes. A book was published in which it was shown how, in remote times, a Lantano-Gunduwian fleet had routed a ragtag fleet of pirate junks ten times stronger in number. And finally it became known that in the stadium of the Lantanian capital a soccer match would take place between each country's best teams.

Bertrando was one of the first to rush out and buy his ticket of admission, but it was already too late: he had to resign himself to spending five times as much buying from the scalpers. It was a splendid day, and the stadium was packed; there was not a breath of wind, and the two flags hung slack from the gigantic masts. At the appointed hour the umpire blew the starting whistle, and at the same instant there rose a sustained breeze. The two flags, side by side for the first time, fluttered gloriously: the Lantanian purple-orange-green next to the Gunduwian's yellow-brown.

Bertrando felt a gelid, searing shiver run down his spine, like a rapier threading his vertebrae. His eyes must be lying, they could not be transmitting to him that double message, that impossible, lacerating yes-no. He experienced revulsion and love to a degree that poisoned him. All around him he saw a crowd, as divided as he, explode. He felt all his muscles contract painfully, adductors and abductors, enemies to each other, the smooth and the striated, and the tireless muscles of the heart; all his glands secreted tumultuously, inundating him with warring hormones. His jaws locked as though from tetanus and he fell to the ground like a block of wood.

May 17, 1984

F I V E   I N T I M A T E
I N T E R V I E W S
■ ■ ■

I

JOURNALIST: Mr. Gull, sir, what are you doing here?
GULL: Herring Gull, if you please. We have a stable status here, it's the others, the black-headed gulls, who are vagabonds, opportunists without scruples.
JOURNALIST: Mr. Herring Gull, sir, I have the impression that I have met you on other occasions, but in a different environment: gliding over the backwash, I don't remember whether at Cinqueterre or at Caprazuppa. But I do remember you executing a fantastic swoop, drifting down on the wind, and then a sudden head-first dive and immediately up with a fish in your beak. I followed it all with my binoculars: I regretted not having a movie camera.
HERRING GULL: In fact, I remember exactly, it was a red mullet, for my nestlings. I'd seen it from above, and I dove two meters under water to catch it. It was quite a coup, I too remember it. Ah, those were the days, but already then the red mullet were becoming rare. My wife and I made for ourselves an inaccessible, almost invisible nest, on

a crag sheer above the water. We lived there without the slightest worry: every foray meant a fish, at times so large that I had trouble carrying it back to the nest, much less swallowing it. That was a worthy, noble trade for those with good wings and a sharp eye. There wasn't a swell that could frighten me—indeed, the stormier it was, the more I felt master of the sky. I've flown amid lightning bolts when even your helicopters were grounded, and I felt happy, "fulfilled," as you would put it.

JOURNALIST: Exactly: an environment fit for a fine flier like you. But what induced you to come and set yourself up at Chivasso?

HERRING GULL: You know, rumors travel. There was a distant relative of mine who lived at Chioggia, and he was doing reasonably well, but then the water turned foamy, it stank of diesel oil, and the fish began dwindling away. At that he and his wife flew up the Po, stage by stage, in fact all the way to Chivasso. Gradually, as they flew farther and farther, the water became less polluted. Well, some years ago he came down there in Liguria to tell me that at Chivasso there is the Lancia factory, and that they employ a lot of people.

JOURNALIST: There's no doubt about that. But are you telling me that they hire gulls too? Or that they are so generous as to supply them with food?

HERRING GULL: You've hit on a sore spot. Obviously, Lancia doesn't manufacture fish, indeed it kills a fair amount of them, but it manufactures waste. It hires people who manufacture an incredible quantity of waste, three or four hundred tons a year. And at Lancia they have a company cafeteria, they manufacture garbage, and with the garbage come . . . yes, come the rats. So there, you made me say it.

JOURNALIST: Are you telling me that you turned yourself from a fisherman into a rat hunter? Ah well, look, these

are things that happen to us too. To men in general, and to
us journalists in particular. It isn't every day nor every year
that we have a war to report on, or a dike that collapses, or
an earthquake, a volcanic eruption, a nuclear catastrophe, a
flight to the moon. At times we too must be satisfied with
running after rats. And if there aren't any, we invent them.
HERRING GULL: . . . or you begin interviewing herring
gulls, right? Anything will do. It's all grist for the mill.
JOURNALIST: No, believe me, I'm fully aware of your
difficulty. One can see, with the naked eye so to speak, that
you no longer fly high in the sky. One rarely hears you
shriek. I have seen two of your colleagues nest at the mouth
of a sewer, others under a bridge. Still others, and many of
them, hang out in the vicinity of the Turin Zoo and steal
fish from the seals and the polar bear.
HERRING GULL: I know. It's shameful. But I went there
too. We need fish; otherwise, our eggs turn out to have a
thin shell, so transparent that you can see the chick inside,
and when you hatch them they break. And when it comes
to fish, you don't see many of them in the Po. Let's hope
that now, with the new treatment plant, the situation will
improve a bit.
JOURNALIST: All the same, considerations of prestige
apart, I should imagine that a nice big rat of the kind that
frequent waste pipe outlets is not a prey to look down your
beak at.
HERRING GULL: And you think that it's easy to catch
a rat? In the beginning the hunt was successful: you saw
something stir among the refuse, you dove down, a good
peck in the neck, and that was the end of the rat. But they
are a fantastically intelligent race, and they immediately
learned how to protect themselves. First of all, they come
out only at night, and we don't see well at night. Then they
post one of their own as a sentinel, and if one of us flies

over the outlet of the sewer, the sentinel sounds the alarm and they all rush into their holes. And, finally, they frighten cats, but they frighten us too, the few times you manage to attack one by surprise and in the open. They have sharp teeth, and such quick reflexes, that quite a few of us have lost lots of feathers, and not only feathers.

JOURNALIST: So all that's left for you is the garbage?

HERRING GULL: You're really intent on rubbing salt in the wound. Garbage, yes. It's not very dignified, but it is beneficial. I too will end up by doing the crows out of their job, and I will get accustomed to eating carrion, bare bones with a few shreds of meat left on them, or perhaps I'll even become a vegetarian. In this world those who don't know how to adapt succumb. On this point I must admit that my wife has fewer scruples than I. When it is my turn to sit on the eggs, she goes walking about the sewer mouth and brings me a bit of everything, so much so that I have to give her a scolding and explain that polyethylene must be left behind, it isn't even good for lining the nest because it isn't porous enough. You should see what she brings me: dead kittens, cabbage stumps, fruit peels, watermelon rinds. There are some things that still turn me off, but the little ones eat everything. The next generation frightens me, all restraint is gone.

JOURNALIST: Sir, you seem too much of a pessimist to me. Just as in England they have cleaned up the Thames, they'll clean up our rivers too, and then even the sea will go back to being what it used to be. In any case, take heart: also among us men there are those who might know how to fly and swim but who, on the contrary, due to bad luck or lack of courage, roam the garbage dumps collecting filth. They will have to be given the opportunity to restore their dignity, and so will you. I beg you, don't forget the sea.

II

JOURNALIST: Just wait a moment, damn it! It's two whole days, forty-eight hours, that I've been waiting here for you to come up, and you already want to go back down inside. Listen, my editor won't take any excuses: if I return without an interview I may lose my job, and he wants it right away, before the mating season.

MOLE: All right then, but hurry up. It's not that I'm in a rush, it's just that I don't like the light. Next time, if you let me know in advance, we'll make an appointment at night, when everything is simpler, and also quieter. Don't you hear the buzz? Tractors, motors, engines, even airplanes in the sky: it's unbearable. Once upon a time, if you go by what they say, it wasn't like this, there was peace out in the fields. But anyway, bear with me, you know I don't see very well: are you male or female?

JOURNALIST: Male, but I don't see what difference it makes.

MOLE: Certainly it makes a difference. You can't trust females. As for me, they interest me only two weeks a year, then nothing, better alone. And the only thing females notice, also your females, is the fur. Not that they're entirely wrong in that: did you know that ours is the only fur that can be stroked also against the grain? Otherwise, we couldn't back up through our tunnels.

JOURNALIST: Tell me, yours was a radical choice. No sky, no sun or moon; in short, perpetual darkness and silence. Isn't that a bit monotonous? Don't you get bored?

MOLE: You're all the same, you measure everything by your human yardstick. It was a choice, yes, but a reasoned choice. I have favored hearing, scent, and touch over sight. Don't think because you can't see them from the outside that I haven't got ears. My hearing is ten times more acute than yours; on a logarithmic scale, of course. I can hear a root grow. I can hear the rustle of a caterpillar. And in order to protect myself from your insufferable racket I have only to descend fifty or sixty centimeters: there I am sure not to freeze. Anything but monotony! I can distinguish at least twenty different types of soil, and I sense humidity and wind before they arrive.

JOURNALIST: Could you show me your front paws, please? I'd like to take a photograph.

MOLE: Certainly not! What is this nonsense? No photos. And why don't you call them hands? After all, they aren't so much different from yours, they're just much more robust. I bet that, big as you are, you could not withstand the tractile force of one of my hands. In any case, look, you try and do what we do every day and every night. It's a while now that it hasn't rained, the soil in my meadow is nice and friable; in short, conditions could not be better. Come on, Mister Man, just renounce for a moment your erect posture, put yourself in a prone position like us, and let's start digging together but without tools. Agreed? Well, you'll see that I, the mole, the slowest of the slow, will have covered ten meters while you will still be breaking your fingernails on the surface. And I will have dug myself a perfect cylindrical tunnel, with the earth well packed against the sides, because ever since I was little I have learned to advance by rotating, like a drill. We too have our trade secrets.

JOURNALIST: You told me that females interest you only a few days out of the year. Do you go looking for them?

MOLE: It's consensual. Females have a completely distinctive scratching style, quicker and softer: we hear them from afar, and they hear us. When it is time for mating, the mutual search is an exalting adventure. It is also a choice: we hear digging above, below, to the east and west, this one cruder, that one smoother, until we decide on the second and then off we go, digging zestfully until the two tunnels meet. Indeed, most of the time we meet nose to nose so that we can also see whether our smells agree: if they do, the marriage is concluded.

JOURNALIST: Would you mind introducing me to your wife?

MOLE: I would do so gladly, because she's a fine girl. Beautiful too: much younger than I. But it's the end of March now, and she has gone somewhere or other to prepare the nuptial chamber. It was very important for me, and I made it clear to her: I wanted it spacious, comfortable, nicely lined with grass and moss, but these are female chores.

JOURNALIST: If you don't mind, what are male chores, according to you?

MOLE: More or less the same as yours: you hunt for money, we hunt for worms. You invest it in commodities or real estate, we cut their heads off.

JOURNALIST: Whose heads? The worms'?

MOLE: Yes, it's the best investment. You wouldn't have thought of it, would you? But an earthworm without its head can't run away and doesn't putrefy. Do you know how many worms I've got in the bank right now? More than eleven hundred, more than forty assorted larvae. After all, one must think of the future, our future and our children's. Once, as I was digging, I even met up with a small, just-hatched viper. I cut off her head too, but two days later it was beginning to stink, and so as not to waste it, I ate it all right away. You know, the strength of our arms has a price: if we don't eat at least our weight in fresh meat every day, it means hunger for us.

JOURNALIST: I see. Just a second and I'll make a note of it. There. But tell me now: aren't you really ever seized by the desire to explore the world on its surface? The grass, the flowers, running water? Or even those other little animals that don't go underground, crickets, snails, grasshoppers?

MOLE: Ah yes, I won't deny it, but those are the exploits of one's youth. I too did all this, with boys of my age, on moonless nights. There were a dozen of us. Just think, one time I found a nightingale's nest just above the ground, with all the eggs inside: what a banquet that was! But the real fun was something else: it was to attract the dogs by scratching hard against a stone, let them come close, poke out with your snout for an instant to scare them, and then pull right back into the burrow. You should have seen how they dug! But we backed up and in a second were out of their reach. In short, if we don't go deliberately looking for trouble, no one bothers us. We live in darkness but also in peace.

III

GIRAFFE: Hey, you down there, what are you looking at? You've been hanging around me for some time now, snapping photos and taking movies. Let me tell you right off, I'm not in a good mood; I don't mean today, I mean ever. With this fence and this metal barrier that keeps me from lowering my head and giving a good taste of my horns to all the pests who come here to go ooh and ahh. One time, however, I did get some satisfaction. One of the visitors was very tall and wore a straw hat. I snatched it off with a lick of my tongue and chewed it up thoroughly. Not that it was good, it tasted of glue, but anyway it was a reprisal.

JOURNALIST: I'm sorry to disturb you. This isn't a whim of mine or of my bosses, but there is talk about disbanding the zoo. You'll end up who knows where, and certain problems that concern you may well remain unsolved.

GIRAFFE: So you're just a journalist in search of strange facts?

JOURNALIST: As for strangeness, consider it a compliment, for you are quite strange.

GIRAFFE: Let's go, then; let's hear your questions, but make them simple, clear, and without traps.

JOURNALIST: Well, let's do it this way: to start in, briefly, sex, height, and weight.

GIRAFFE: The fact is, I'm a male—not that I'm trying to boast, though I think that's visible even from a distance.

JOURNALIST: Of course. I asked that only for the record. With such a long neck, how many cervical vertebrae do you have?

GIRAFFE: I have seven vertebrae, exactly the same as you and as a mouse. I weigh seven hundred kilos, and my height is six meters, twenty centimeters.

JOURNALIST: I see. This means that with your head held high you exert a spectacular pressure on your hoofs; [he takes a pad and pencil from his pocket] when you figure it out, something like four hundred fifty millimeters of mercury plus at least another one hundred forty supplied by the heart. A total, let us say, of six hundred, while we with two hundred are already not doing so well; and yet we are mammals, both you and we, and we are made more or less of the same materials. Don't you suffer from hypertension, especially when you run? Or from varicose veins or internal hemorrhages?

GIRAFFE: You should know that ever since we decided to lengthen our neck and legs so as to be able to browse on the highest leaves, we have always cultivated hydrostatics, physiology, and histology with intelligence and passion. We immediately realized that certain innovations entail problems; for example, the act of drinking is no small problem for us. In the first place, even when we lower our necks to their entire length, we do not reach level with the ground. Thus, as soon as our little ones are weaned, we must teach them that in order to drink from rivers, it is necessary to spread the front legs quite a bit. It's not elegant, but it's necessary. And then you must get the water to reach a height of approximately three meters. We understood immediately that the pump of the glottis did not suffice; so then our sages solved the problem by presenting us with a series of small peristaltic pumps arranged along the esophagus.

Despite all this, I cannot say that drinking is for us the easiest undertaking in the world; in fact, I personally am grateful to the zoo's director, who has installed for me that funny watering trough you see there, which you would not be able to touch with your hand even if you stood on tiptoe. So, due to the complicated preparations, we drink rarely, and as much as possible each time.

JOURNALIST: Thank you. But we still have to define the matter of the feet: I mean the disparity in pressure between when you lie down and stand up.

GIRAFFE: We never lie down: we leave such weaknesses to the cows and to you. We sleep on our feet, always ready to flee. Because we have many enemies.

JOURNALIST: But what about hypertension? I mean . . .

GIRAFFE: Judging by your insistence, you really seem to have a personal problem there.

JOURNALIST: Well, yes, actually . . . hypotensives, diuretics, no salt . . . It's not a simple life.

GIRAFFE: That's all because you didn't equip yourself in due time. As for us, we have hypertension, but it doesn't bother us at all. Did you ever wear an elastic bandage? Well, on our four legs we have elastic bandages that are congenital and incorporated. I can tell you that they are very comfortable: veins and arteries do not distend, even though the pressure is as high as you have calculated; and they are made of first-rate material, which does not wear out and indeed is renewed in the course of time.

■ ■ ■

Furthermore, we've found a way to reduce the pressure of reflux blood. With you the blood of the arteries is heavy, but so is that of the veins, which must flow back up to the heart. Well, we have perfected a line of small valves arranged inside all the large veins that bear upward traffic. These valves open with every pulsation and close again, preventing the blood from burdening the vascular system. It's as though each vein were subdivided into independent segments. You must forgive my primitive language, I'm not a physiologist, I'm only a male giraffe proud of his stature and humiliated by captivity. But enough now, please, I must have a bit of exercise. It's not that the vet prescribed it, it's instinct and nature. I must run, even though only inside the miserable space in which you have confined me.

JOURNALIST: [picks up pad and writes] "Despite their structure, so different from that of other quadrupeds, giraffes when running are extraordinarily elegant. Their gait is halfway between gallop and dance. The four hoofs leave the ground almost simultaneously, while the neck balances the majestic rhythm of their progress. It seems slow, yet it is very swift: it brings to mind the sailing of a ship and does not reveal the slightest effort. The vast body sways quite naturally, tilting toward the inside when the animal curves its path. In observing this, I have realized how great their need is for the freedom of open spaces and how cruel it is to restrict them within the mesh of a fence. And yet the specimen I interviewed was born here, in captivity, ignorant of the untouched splendor of the savannah, but bears within him a primordial nobility." [He reads the text aloud.]

GIRAFFE: Grunt!

IV

JOURNALIST: Good evening, Mr. Spider, or rather, Mrs. Spider.

SPIDER: [in a strident voice] Are you edible?

JOURNALIST: Well, I think I am, but this is a matter that's never come up.

SPIDER: You know, we have quite a number of eyes, but we are very short-sighted, and we're hungry all the time. For us the world is divided into two parts: things you can eat, and the rest.

JOURNALIST: You see, I'm here not as a potential victim but for an interview.

SPIDER: An interview? Can you eat interviews? Are they nutritious? If they are, do it right away; apart from all else, my curiosity is aroused, during my life I've eaten a bit of everything but never an interview. How many legs do they have? Do they have wings?

JOURNALIST: No, they're not actually eaten, but they are consumed in a different manner. How shall I put it? Simply, they have readers, and at times they nourish them a little bit.

SPIDER: In that case the matter doesn't interest me much; but if you promise to pay me with a few flies or a couple of mosquitoes . . . You know, with the hygiene that there is nowadays they've become quite scarce. Are you good at catching flies? Big as you are, it shouldn't be difficult for you: I can't imagine how large your web must be.

JOURNALIST: To tell the truth, we use different methods, and besides, catching flies is not an occupation that takes up much of our time. We eat flies unwillingly and only by accident. At any rate, it's agreed: I'll do my best. So may I begin? Tell me, why do you hang with your head down?

SPIDER: To concentrate. I have only a few thoughts, and like this they flow into my brain and I see things more clearly. But don't come so close, and be careful with that gadget you're holding; I wouldn't want it to tear my web: I made a new one just this morning. It had only a very small hole (beetles aren't very considerate, you know), but with us it's perfection or nothing. At the very first flaw I eat up the web again, digest it, and then have the material ready to make myself another one. It's a matter of principle. Our mind is a bit limited, but our patience is boundless. I've even had to do the web over as many as three times in one day, but that was an unprecedented effort. After the third web, which fortunately nobody spoiled, I had to take a rest for three or four days. Everything takes time, even the business of filling the spinnery glands; but as I was telling you, we have a lot of patience, and to wait is no trouble at all for us. When you wait, you don't consume energy.

JOURNALIST: I've seen your webs, they're masterpieces, but do you make them all the same? Never an improvement, never an innovation?

SPIDER: You mustn't ask too much of us. Look, for me it is already an effort to answer your questions; we have no imagination, we are not inventors, our cycle is simplified. Hunger, web, flies, digestion, hunger, new web. And so why should we rack our brains—forgive me, our nervous ganglia—to come up with new webs? We're better off entrusting ourselves to the memory we carry imprinted inside, the immemorial model, trying at most to adapt it to the contours we happen to have at our disposal. For our intelligence, that's already too much. If I remember correctly, I had been hatched from the egg only a few days before I made my first web; it was the size of a postage stamp, but aside from its scale, it was identical with this one right in front of your nose.

JOURNALIST: I see. Now tell me, there are rumors abroad concerning your, let us say, matrimonial behavior . . . only rumors, let's be clear about it, I personally have never seen anything objectionable, but as you know, people will gossip . . .

SPIDER: Are you alluding to the fact that we eat the male? Is that all? But of course, certainly. It's a sort of ballet; our males are rather skinny, timid, and weak, they aren't even all that good at making a proper web. When they are overcome by desire, they venture onto our web step by step, uncertain, hesitant, because they too know how it will end up. We wait for them: we don't take the initiative, the game is clear to both parties. We females like the males as much as flies, if not more. We like them in every sense of the word, as husbands (but only for the minimum indispensable length of time) and as food. Once they have fulfilled their function, they lose all appeal except that of fresh meat; and so, in a single stroke, we fill our stomach and matrix.

JOURNALIST: Do the marriages always end like this?

SPIDER: Not always. Some males have foresight, they know about our unrelenting hunger, and they bring us a nuptial gift. Not out of affection or as a compliment, you understand, but only to satiate us: a daddy longlegs, a gnat, even at times something more substantial, and in that case everything goes smoothly and all they suffer is anxiety. You ought to see them, the wretches, as they sit there waiting to see whether their gift has been enough to gratify us; and sometimes, if it seems to them it wasn't enough, they rush back to their web to fetch another tidbit.

JOURNALIST: This seems to me a rather ingenious system, and as a whole it follows a certain logic. I too in their place would act like that, but, you see, my wife has a smaller appetite and a milder temperament; and besides, our marriages last for a long time, to us it would seem a pity to be content with a single copulation.

SPIDER: To each his own, obviously, but I meant to tell you that this is not the only system the males have invented so as not to be devoured. There are others, some distant cousins of ours, who pretend to be dancing a dance of joy around the female they have chosen, and meanwhile they're tying her up little by little, securely interweaving the threads, then they fertilize her and leave. And others yet fear our strength; they come and steal the just-hatched females, still adolescent and not very dangerous, and they keep them sequestered in some crack until puberty, feeding them, true enough, but the barest possible minimum so that they remain alive without gathering too much strength. Then they too do their job, free the girls, and rush off.

JOURNALIST: Thank you. The interview is over.

SPIDER: Thank goodness, I was beginning to feel tired: intellectual activity was never my strong point. But don't forget the flies: every promise is a debt.

V

JOURNALIST: [knocks delicately at the intestinal wall] May I come in?

ESCHERICHIA COLI*: Yes! Come in.

JOURNALIST: Now, look, there won't be any bloodshed, I have no intention of harming your host, who besides all else is a friend of mine. No drastic intervention: if you agree, we'll do the interview like this: from the outside to the inside. I'm recording it, and the microphone is very

* A form of intestinal bacteria discovered by Dr. Theodor Escherich (1857–1911). —TRANS.

sensitive, just try to speak a bit louder. Is this the first time you've been interviewed?

E. COLI: Yes, but don't worry, I'm not at all nervous. We do not have an emotional temperament, both by natural disposition and because we are not provided with a nervous system.

JOURNALIST: Do you like it down there in the dark, surrounded by all that half-digested stuff that your host drops on your head three or four times a day?

E. COLI: Well enough, except when they give him some sort of antibiotics. Then our life becomes a bit rough, but a few of us always get away, and we almost always manage to perpetuate the race. Now bear with me for a moment, I'm in mitosis, I mean to say I'm splitting up: but it won't take more than a few minutes, then one of my halves will again be at your disposal . . . There, it's done, you can go ahead, I'll stay here and my twin will go her way. She won't stay to listen, and she won't disturb us; we know how to be discreet.

JOURNALIST: As I'm sure you know, you're no longer just any saprophyte,* tolerated as long as you don't give us a bellyache. By now you've made the front pages in the newspapers; we've learned how to remove a fragment of your DNA and replace it with another, and so we teach you how to produce the proteins that are convenient for us. On this subject there have been discordant opinions; there are those who say that everything is going well, that indeed in this manner we will be able to teach you bacteria even how to fix atmospheric nitrogen; and there are those who are afraid that you might learn too much, that you will end up by taking over.

---

* Any vegetable organism that lives on decayed organic matter. — TRANS.

E. COLI: Yes, yes, I'm aware of all that. Actually, a three-hundred-ninety-seventh cousin of mine was operated on exactly in this way, and she didn't even suffer very much, aside from the trauma at finding herself surrounded by a glass tube instead of a nice, warm intestine. Well, I'm a member of the Prokaryocytes* Workers' Council, and from a union point of view we have no objections. The times of egalitarian demands have passed: we've understood that for us too specialization is indispensable, and advantageous to both parties. In fact, for quite some time now we have ceased to go out on strike, and I, as a representative of the category, consider that at this point strikes have become a blunt weapon: the opposite party disposes of excessively powerful means. By its very nature, politics is the art of the possible. Precisely because of this you mustn't underestimate us. Listen to my advice: keep an eye on your test tubes. I personally have a good disposition, but I cannot vouch for those colleagues of mine whose switchboard you have changed. You will have to guarantee them; so just watch out. If an epidemic should be unleashed, you would bear the brunt of it, but so would we who peacefully live in your precious entrails. There is no doubt that in the long run we would learn how to adjust so as to survive even in the intestine of a cockroach or an oyster, but it would take time and effort and a good number of casualties.

JOURNALIST: Madame, I thank you. If you have nothing else to add, I'll end the interview here.

E. COLI: This is really too much! And what about the invention of the wheel and the synchronous engine? You took two hundred years to become aware of it, since you

---

* Prokaryocyte, an organism whose cells do not have a morphologically distinct nucleus, since they lack the nuclear membrane, like viruses, bacteria, and blue algae.

set up the first microscope, but now our priority is acknowledged; and you come here to me with your microphone and don't say a word about it? Believe me, this is incredible. It's your arrogance as multicellulars: as though you had discovered everything!

JOURNALIST: You must forgive me. You know, we journalists must deal with so many things—Craxi's courier, the tax on health, Lebanon, Reagan's last blunder . . .

E. COLI: Are you saying that you know nothing about it? Pay attention, I'll explain it to you in two minutes so you won't make a mistake in your reportage. We have six flagella, or antennae, right? But we do not agitate them as you would agitate a rope or a whip. We whirl them, just like the rotor in a small electric engine. For each flagellum we have a motor and a stator, each flagellum becomes an elongated coil, all six of them arrange themselves in a sort of tuft and push us forward like a propeller when we smell food. Quite simple, isn't it?

Then came the ciliates, which are something else altogether, the wheel was forgotten, and it took two billion years for you to rediscover it and come up with your wagons; and the first were war wagons, or am I mistaken?

JOURNALIST: I thank you, that's very interesting information. You mean to say that if the ciliates hadn't popped up, with their cells and their silly alternate motor, we today could turn our heads three hundred sixty degrees, or even three thousand six hundred degrees, without ever going back? And what are we to do with blood vessels, nerves, and all the rest of it? They'd all get twisted up.

E. COLI: That's your problem—or, more precisely, evolution's problem. But your autos work fine, and that's exactly how they're made. What I mean to say is that you have let

an idea go to waste that was quite remarkable. A pity it's
now a bit too late to take a patent out on it.

I: January 14, 1987
II and V: November 17, 1986
III: February 1, 1987
IV: February 26, 1987

THE MIRROR MAKER
∎ ∎ ∎

Timoteo, his father, and all his ancestors back to the remotest times, had always made mirrors. In a bread chest in their house were still kept copper mirrors, green from oxidation, and silver mirrors blackened by centuries of human emanations; there were others made of crystal and framed with ivory or precious wood. After his father died, Timoteo felt himself freed from the shackles of tradition; he continued to fashion mirrors according to the rules of the trade, which in any case he sold profitably throughout the region, but he also began once more to think about an old plan of his.

Even as a boy, unbeknownst to his father and his grandfather, he had broken the guild's rules. By day, during the hours in the workshop, being a disciplined apprentice, he made the usual boring, flat mirrors: transparent, colorless, the kind that, as the saying goes, reflect the truthful (though virtual) image of the world, and especially the image of human faces. In the evening, when nobody watched him, he concocted a different kind of mirror. What does a mirror do? "It reflects," like a human mind; but the ordinary run of mirrors obey a simple and inexorable physical law; they reflect as would a rigid, obsessed mind that claims to gather in itself *the* reality of the world—as though there were only one! Timoteo's secret mirrors were more versatile.

Some were of colored, striated, milky glass: they reflected a world that was redder or greener than the real one, or multicolored, or with delicately shaded contours so that objects or persons seemed to agglomerate like clouds. Some were multiple, made of ingeniously angled thin plates or shards: these shattered the image, reduced it to a graceful but indecipherable mosaic. A device, which had cost Timoteo weeks of work, inverted the high and the low, and right and left; whoever looked into it for the first time experienced intense dizziness, but if he persevered for a few hours he ended by getting used to the world upside down and then felt nauseous, confronted by a world suddenly straightened out. Another mirror was made of three leaves, and anyone who looked at himself in it would see his face multiplied by three: Timoteo gave it as a present to the parish priest so that during the catechism hour he could explain to the children the mystery of the Trinity.

There were mirrors that enlarged, as it is foolishly said the eyes of oxen do, others that made smaller or made things appear infinitely distant; in some of them you saw yourself tall and lanky, in others obese and short, like Buddha. With the idea of giving a present to Agatha, Timoteo used for a wardrobe mirror a slightly undulated sheet of glass, but he obtained a result that he had not foreseen. If the subject looked at himself without moving, the image showed only slight deformities; if instead the subject moved up and down, slightly flexing the knees or rising on tiptoe, belly and chest impetuously flowed up or down. Agatha saw herself transformed into a stork-woman, with shoulders, breast, and abdomen compressed into a bundle balanced on two extremely long, sticklike legs; and immediately after into a monster with a thread of a neck from which hung all the rest, a mass of hernias squashed and squat like potter's clay that folds up under its own weight. The story ended badly. Agatha broke mirror and engagement, and Timoteo was hurt, but not too much.

He had a more ambitious project in mind. In great secrecy he tested various types of glass and silver plating, he subjected his mirrors to electric fields, irradiated them with lamps he had sent to him from distant countries, until it seemed to him that he was close to his goal, which was to develop metaphysical mirrors. A Metamir, that is, a metaphysical mirror, does not obey the laws of optics but reproduces your image as it is seen by the person who stands before you: the idea was old, Aesop had already had it, and who knows how many others before and after him, but Timoteo had been the first to realize it.

Timoteo's Metamirs were the size of a calling card, flexible, and adhesive: in fact they were meant to be applied to the forehead. Timoteo tested the first specimen by gluing it to the wall, and in it he saw nothing special: his usual image of an already balding thirty-year-old with a witty, dreamy, and slightly neglected air: but of course a wall does not see you, does not harbor images of you. He prepared about twenty samples, and it seemed right to him that he should offer the first to Agatha, with whom he had maintained a tempestuous relationship, hoping that she might forgive him for that matter of the wavy mirror.

Agatha received him coldly; she listened to his explanation with ostentatious inattention, but when Timoteo suggested that she attach the Metamir to her brow, she readily agreed: she had understood even too well Timoteo's thought. Indeed, the image of himself that he saw, as on a small video screen, was not very flattering. His hairline was not just receding, he was bald, his lips hung half open in a foolish smirk that revealed his rotten teeth (true, for quite some time now he had kept putting off the treatment advised by the dentist), his expression was not dreamy but positively moronic, and the look in his eyes was very strange indeed. Why strange? He soon understood: in a normal mirror your eyes are always looking at you, whereas in that mirror they looked obliquely toward his left. He approached and moved a little to one side: the eyes snapped, escaping to the right. Timoteo left Agatha with conflicting feelings: the experiment had been successful, but if Agatha truly saw him like that, the break could only be definitive.

He offered a second Metamir to his mother, who did not ask for explanations. He saw himself as a sixteen-year-old, blond, pink, ethereal, and angelic, his hair well combed and the knot of his tie set just so: like an *in memoriam* photo, he thought to himself. Nothing in common with the school photograph he'd found in a drawer a few years before, which showed a lively little boy, but interchangeable with the majority of his schoolmates.

The third Metamir belonged to Emma, no doubt about it. Timoteo had slid from Agatha to Emma without undue jolts. Emma was tiny, lazy, mild, and sly. Under the covers she had taught Timoteo certain skills that he by himself would never have thought of. She was less intelligent than Agatha, but she did not possess her stony hardness. Agate-Agatha: Timoteo had never noticed this before, names do after all stand for something. Emma understood nothing about Timoteo's work, but she often knocked at his workshop door and stayed there watching him for hours on end with an enchanted gaze. On Emma's smooth brow Timoteo saw a marvelous Timoteo. He was half length, his torso bare: he had the well-proportioned chest that he had always regretted not having, an Apollo-like face framed by a thick mane of hair in which you could glimpse a wreath of laurel, a gaze that was at once serene, merry, and hawklike. At that very moment Timoteo realized that he loved Emma with an intense, tender, and enduring love.

He distributed several Metamirs to his friends. He noticed that no two images coincided: in short, a real Timoteo did not exist. He further noticed that the Metamir possessed a conspicuous virtue: it reinforced old and serious friendships, it rapidly dissolved friendships that were due to habit and convention. Nevertheless, every attempt at commercial exploitation failed: all the salesmen agreed in reporting that customers satisfied with their image as reflected on the brow of friends or relations were too few. In any case, the sales would have been very small, even if the price were to be halved. Timoteo patented his Metamir and bled himself white for several years in an attempt to keep the patent alive, he tried in vain to sell it, then he resigned himself and continued to make flat mirrors, which were indeed of excellent quality, until the age of retirement.

November 1, 1985

THROUGH THE WALLS
. . .

Memnone had lost count of the days and years. Of the four walls within which he was confined he knew every wrinkle, crack, and knob: he had studied them with his eyes by day, with his fingers by night. He continually fingered the stone, from the floor up to where his arms could reach, as though he were reading and rereading the same book: an alchemist always learns something from matter, and at any rate he had nothing else to read.

It was precisely his art that had put him in jail. The guild was powerful, strict in its orthodoxy, recognized by the Emperor, and its dictate was clear: matter is infinitely divisible. Its image was water, not sand; to maintain that there exist those ultimate granules, the atoms, was heresy. Would anyone who spent his life dividing water in the end encounter a barrier? Now Memnone had dared to think he would, and had proclaimed, written, and taught this to his disciples. He would not be released until he recanted.

He could not recant. His mind's eye told him that matter was vacuous and sparse, like the star-studded sky; minuscule granules suspended in the void, governed by hatred and love. That is why they had walled him in alive, so that the ruthless hardness and impenetrability of stone would speak up and confute him; but Memnone knew that the stone was lying, and he knew that this was the core of the art, to give the lie to the lie. He remembered what he had seen in his workshop. Air, water, and sesame seeds will pass through a sieve. Air and water will pass through a piece of felt, but the sesame seed will not. Air but not water passes through leather. From a well-sealed amphora neither air nor water can escape. But he was certain that there existed a more subtle air, an ether capable of passing through hardened clay, bronze, and the stone that buried him; and that his very own body could become thin enough to penetrate the stone.

How? *"Homo est quod est"*—"Man is what he eats": obese and rustic if he eats fatback, valiant if he eats bread, placid if he eats oil, weak if he eats only turnips. Now the food handed to him through the peephole was crude, but he would be able to refine it. He ripped off a strip from his mantle, filled it with the dust that covered the floor, spreading it out in gradual and skillful stages, and made a filter with it, according to a design that only he and Hecate knew. From then on he filtered the slop, discarding its denser parts. After a few months—or perhaps it was a year?—the effects of all this became noticeable. At first it was only a great weakness, but then he saw, in the light from the tiny window, that his hand was becoming increasingly diaphanous until he could make out its bones, which were also tenuous.

He began the test. He rested the tip of one finger against the wall and pushed. He felt a prickling and saw that the finger was penetrating. This was a double victory: the confirmation of his vision and the door to freedom. He waited for a moonless night, then pressed the palms of both hands with all his strength; they entered, though with difficulty; also his arms went in. He pushed with his forehead, felt it fuse with the stone, progress very slowly, and at the same time he was invaded by nausea: it was a painful sensation, he perceived the stone in his brain and his brain commingled with the stone.

He concentrated the effort in his arms, as if he were swimming in tar, amidst a buzzing that deafened him and a darkness broken by inexplicable flashes, until he felt his feet leave the floor. How thick was the wall? About two meters perhaps: the outer surface could not be far. He soon realized that his right hand had emerged: he felt it move freely in the air, but he had trouble extricating the rest of his body from the stone's viscosity. He could not push against the wall on the outside: his hands were caught again in the glue. He felt like a fly caught in honey, which in order to free one little leg traps another two, but he propelled himself forcefully with his legs, and in the first light of dawn he emerged into the air like a butterfly from its pupa.

He let himself fall to the ground, from a height of about twelve feet; he did not hurt himself, but he was still drenched in stone, stony, hindered. He must hide immediately. He walked laboriously, but not only from weakness and the effort of his passage. His body, emaciated though it was, still weighed enough so that the soles of his feet penetrated into the ground. He found grass and walked more easily; then, again, the town's paving stones. He realized that, despite his weariness, it was best for him to run, so as not to give his feet the time to get caught: run without ever stopping. Until when? Was this freedom? Was this its price?

He found Hecate. She had waited for him, but she was an old woman: she asked him to sit down and let him speak;

and, filled with fear, he immediately felt his buttocks fuse
with the chair's wood, he found he could rest only on the
bed, with his weight distributed among the quilt's feathers.
He explained to the woman that he must take nourishment
in order to densify again, to reestablish the borders between
himself and the world; or would it not be better to wait so
as to defeat his adversaries with the proof of fact? Matter,
even his, was penetrable, therefore discrete, therefore made
of atoms: no one could contradict him without contradicting
himself.

Hunger prevailed. Hecate offered food to Memnone
as he lay there: shoulder of mutton, legumes. The mutton
was leathery, and he could not chew it. Jaw, meat, and man-
dible got stuck to each other; he was afraid that his teeth
would be pulled out of their sockets. Hecate had to help
him, using the point of the knife as a lever. For the time
being it was better to take milk, eggs, and fresh cheese: that
extenuated body could not endure pressures, and yet, after
such long abstinence, it swelled with desire. Memnone drew
the woman into the bed, undressed her, and just as, a few
hours earlier, he had explored the stone of the jail, he explored her skin: it had remained young, he felt it soft,
smooth, and perfumed. He embraced the woman, delighted
at that reawakened vigor: it was an unforeseen effect, a marginal but felicitous product of his subtileness; or perhaps it
was a residual stoniness, hard atoms of stone commingled
with his atoms of flesh and undefeated spirit.

Carried away by desire, he had forgotten his new condition. He clasped the woman tightly and felt his separate-
ness dissolve into hers, the two skins confluent and melting.
For an instant or forever? In a twilight of consciousness he
tried to detach himself and pull back, but Hecate's arms, so
much stronger than his, imprisoned him. He again experi-

enced the dizziness that had seized him while he was moving through the stone: no longer irritating now but delicious and mortal. He dragged the woman along with him into a perpetual night of impossibility.

March 2, 1986

THE ANT'S WEDDING
. . .

JOURNALIST: My dear lady, I see that you are very busy. I hope I am not disturbing you: for someone like me this is a rare occasion.

QUEEN: It's what you call a scoop, right? Well, first of all get out from under my feet. I mean: remove your feet. You're ruining the cupola; it will take at least three thousand ant hours to repair the damage you've already done. Our cupolas are either perfect or they're nothing. That's how we, and I in particular, are. There, that's a good girl. Now let's go on. Yes, you may use the recorder. By the way, why no "Majesty"? How do you address your queens?

JOURNALIST: Forgive me, madam, I mean forgive me, Your Majesty. I thought that . . .

QUEEN: There isn't much for you to think about. Perhaps because I'm a widow and I'm laying eggs? Well? Precisely because of this. Can you find me a human queen capable of accomplishing as much? Majesty! Obviously I'm a majesty. Do you know how many eggs I've laid so far? A million and a half, and I'm only fourteen years old, and I've made love only once.

JOURNALIST: Would you like to tell us something about your wedding?

QUEEN: It was a splendid afternoon, full of colors, perfumes, and poetry: one of those moments when it seems the world is singing. It had just stopped raining, and the sun had come back out, and I felt a desire, an irresistible impulsion, the muscles of my wings were so turgid they seemed about to burst. Oh, when you're young . . . My husband, God bless his soul, was very strong and charming: I immediately liked his smell and he liked mine. He pursued me for a good half hour, insistently, and—well, you know how we females are, I pretended I was tired and let him catch me, though I too was a splendid flier. Yes, it was unforgettable, you're free to write that in your paper: from up there you could no longer even see our anthills, his and mine. And he, poor thing, handed me the little parcel and immediately plunged down stone dead: not even the time to say our farewells.

JOURNALIST: . . . the little parcel?

QUEEN: The kind of parcel you don't often see, with more than four million tiny beasts, all of them vital. Since then I've been keeping it in my abdomen. I work with pump and faucet, because we have them incorporated: for each egg three or four spermatozoa, and when I want male children all I have to do is shut off the conduit. Believe me, we've never been able to understand your system. I mean, the honeymoon is fine, but after that what's the need for all those repeat performances? All lost working hours. You'll see that with time you too will get there, just as you've gotten to a division of labor: for people fertility is just waste and demagogy. You too ought to delegate it, you too after all have kings and queens, or even only presidents; leave it to them, the workers must work.

And why so many men? This fifty-fifty of yours is obsolete, let me tell you; it isn't for nothing that our regime has lived for 150 million years, and yours not even one million. Ours is tried and tested, it's been stable since the Mesozoic, while you change every twenty years, if you're lucky. Look, I don't want to interfere in your affairs, and I realize that anatomy and physiology are difficult to renew over the short term, but even the way matters stand with you at present, one male for every fifty females would be abundantly sufficient. Besides all else, you would solve the world hunger problem.

JOURNALIST: And what about the other forty-nine?

QUEEN: It would be best for them not to be born. Otherwise, one would just have to see: kill them, or castrate them, or put them to work, or let them kill each other, considering that they have that tendency. Talk about it with your publisher, write an editorial; it's a bill that should be introduced in parliament.

JOURNALIST: I'll definitely talk to him about it. But, Your Majesty, didn't you ever yearn for that afternoon, that flight, that instant of love?

QUEEN: It's hard to say. You see, for us beauty comes before all else; and anyway, when all is said and done, I'm doing quite nicely here in the dark, the warmth and peace, surrounded by my hundred thousand daughters, who lick me all day long. There is a time for everything, one of your people said so many centuries back: it seems to me that he also invited you to imitate us. For us this is a strict rule, there's a time for eggs, another for the larvae, still another for the pupae; there are day and night, summer and winter, war and peace, work and fertility: but above all there is the State and nothing outside the State.

Well, as for yearnings, certainly. I told you I was a great flier: perhaps it is because of this that my poor husband had chosen precisely me from among the crowd of princesses that swarmed in the sunset. We were so many that we obscured the sun: from a distance it seemed that a column of smoke was issuing from the anthill, but I was the one who flew higher than all of them. I had the musculature of an athlete. And he pursued me, he entrusted me with that gift that contained all our tomorrows, and then immediately down he went: I see him even now, he fell in a spiral like a leaf.

JOURNALIST: And what about you, Your Majesty?

QUEEN: That little parcel is a responsibility, and it's heavy—also materially. I went back down, in fact I let myself fall: a bit out of weariness and a bit from distress. No longer a virgin aviatrix but a widowed mother, gravid with millions. The first thing to do when you become a mother is to get rid of the wings: they are a frivolity, vanity, and in any event they are no longer needed. I immediately tore them off, and I dug out a niche for myself, as has been done since always. I was tempted to keep them in my cell as a souvenir, but then I thought that that too was vanity, and I left them there for the wind to carry away. I could feel the eggs as they matured inside me, thick as hail. When this moment arrives, the muscles for the wings become providential in another way. I assimilated, consumed, incorporated them in order to have the substance to transfer to the eggs, to my future people. To it I sacrificed my strength and my youth, and I am proud of it. I, I alone. There are races that keep in their nests as many as twenty queens: that is something shameful that was never seen among us. Let one of my workers just try and become fertile, and she'll see!

JOURNALIST: I understand. To generate is a total commitment. I understand that you should lay claim to its monopoly. Maternity is sacred among us too, did you know that? Our crime news pages are full of horrors, but whoever harms the little ones is execrated by everyone.

QUEEN: Yes, yes, you mustn't eat the eggs, it's not nice. But there are situations in which one must follow the sense of the State, which after all is good common sense. When food is scarce and eggs are too many, there is no room for moralisms. We eat the eggs, and I'm the first—even the larvae and the pupae. They are nutritious; and if they're left there uncared for, because the workers are hungry and can no longer work, they go bad, they're good only for the worms, and we too will die. So what? Without logic there is no government.

April 20, 1986

FORCE MAJEURE
■ ■ ■

M. was in a hurry because he had an important appointment with the manager of a library. He was not familiar with that section of town; he asked a passerby for the street, and the man pointed to a long, narrow alleyway. Its pavement was cobbled. M. entered it, and when he had gone halfway down it he saw a husky lad in a T-shirt, perhaps a sailor, come toward him. He was disturbed to notice that there were neither niches nor doorways: even though M. was slim, when they would cross he would be forced to make a disagreeable contact. The sailor whistled, M. heard a bark at his back, the scraping of claws, then the panting of the excited animal: the dog must have squatted down to wait.

They both advanced until they came face to face. M. moved close to the wall to free the passage, but the other did not do the same; he stopped and placed his hands on his hips, completely obstructing the path. He did not have a threatening expression; he seemed to be calmly waiting, but M. heard the dog let out a deep snarl: it must be a large animal. He took a step forward, and at that the man put his hands against the walls. There was a brief pause, then the sailor made a gesture with both his palms turned down, as though he were stroking a long back or calming the waters. M. did not understand; he asked, "Why don't you let me go through?" But the other answered by repeating the gesture. Perhaps he was mute, or deaf, or did not understand Italian: but he should have been able to understand, the question was not that complex.

Without warning, the sailor slipped off M.'s eyeglasses, stuffed them into M.'s pocket, and delivered a punch to his stomach: not very hard, but M., taken by surprise, backed up several paces. He had never found himself in a similar situation, not even as a boy, but he remembered Martin Eden and his encounter with Cheese Face, he had read *Ettore Fieramosca, Orlando Innamorato, Orlando Furioso, Gerusalemme*, and *Don Quixote*, he remembered the story of Fra Cristoforo in *The Betrothed*, he had seen *The Quiet Man, High Noon*, and a hundred other films, and so he knew that sooner or later, for him too, the moment would come: it comes for everyone. He tried to screw up his courage and answered with a straight punch but realized with astonishment that his arm was too short: he wasn't even able to graze the face of his opponent, who had kept him at a distance by propping his hands against M.'s shoulders. At that he charged the sailor with his head low: not only was it a matter of dignity and pride, not only did he have to get through, but at that moment getting down that alley seemed to him a matter of life or death. The young man caught M.'s head between his hands, pushed him back, and repeated the gesture with the palms of his hands, which M. glimpsed through the haze of his myopia.

It crossed M.'s mind that he too could make a surprise move: he had never learned any kind of combat, but he had after all retained something from his reading, and there flashed through his mind, from a remote part, a sentence read thirty years before in a novel about the savage North: "If your opponent is stronger than you, crouch down, hurl yourself against his legs, and crack his knees." He drew back a few steps, got up speed, bunched up in a ball, and rolled against the sailor's sturdy legs. The sailor lowered a hand, only one, stopped M. without effort, grabbed him by one arm, and lifted him to his feet: he had a surprised expression on his face. Then he again made the same gesture. Meanwhile the dog had approached and was sniffing at M.'s pants with a menacing air. M. heard a sharp, resonant step behind him: it was a girl in gaudy clothes, perhaps a prostitute. She went past the dog, M., and the sailor as though she did not see them, and disappeared at the end of the alley. M., who until then had lived a normal life strewn with joys, irritations and sorrows, successes and failures, perceived a sensation he had never experienced before, that of persecution, *force majeure*, absolute impotence, without escape or remedy, to which one can react only by submission. Or with death: but was there any sense in dying just to pass through an alley-way?

Suddenly the sailor caught him by the shoulders and pushed him down: his strength was really extraordinary, and M. was forced to kneel on the cobbles, but the other continued to push. M. felt an intolerable pain in his knees; he tried to transfer part of his weight to his heels, and to do so he had to get down even lower and bend backward. The sailor took advantage of this: his push changed from vertical to oblique, and M. found himself sitting with his arms propped behind him. This position was more stable, but because M. was now much lower, the other person's pressure against his shoulders had become proportionally more intense. Slowly, with convulsed and useless attempts at resistance, M. found himself leaning on his elbows, then stretched out, but with his knees bent and high: at least that. They were made of hard, rigid bone, difficult to defeat.

The youth gave a sigh, as one who must gather all his patience, seized M.'s heels one at a time, and straightened out his legs against the ground by pressing on the kneecaps. So that was the meaning of the gesture, M. thought: the sailor wanted him lying down, right away; he could not tolerate any sort of resistance. The man chased away the dog with a curt command, took off his sandals, and, holding them in his hands, prepared to walk along M.'s body as you walk down the balancing beam in the gym: slowly, arms outstretched, staring straight ahead. He placed one foot on the right tibia, then the other on the left femur, and in succession on the liver, the left side of the chest, the right shoulder, finally the forehead. He slipped on his sandals and left, followed by the dog.

M. got to his feet, put on his glasses, and straightened his clothes. He made a rapid inventory: were there side advantages, advantages that someone trampled on derived from his condition? Compassion, sympathy, greater attention, less responsibility? No, because M. lived alone. There weren't any, nor would there be any; or, if so, they would be minimal. The duel had not resembled its models: it had been unbalanced, unfair, dirty, and had dirtied him. The models, even the most violent, are chivalrous; life is not. He set out for his appointment, knowing that he would never be the same man as before.

July 27, 1986

A MYSTERY IN
THE *LAGER*
∎ ∎ ∎

In November 1944 we had a Dutch *Kapo* who in civilian life had played the trumpet in a small orchestra in an Amsterdam café. As a *Musiker*, he was part of the camp's band, and was therefore a somewhat anomalous *Kapo* with two functions, so that at the end of the prisoners' march to work he had to get off the platform, put away his trumpet, and run after the column to take his place. He was a vulgar man, but not particularly violent; well fed, stupidly proud of his almost clean striped pajamas, to which his function entitled him, and extremely partial toward his Dutch subjects, of whom there were four or five in our squad of about seventy prisoners.

When New Year approached, in order to further ingratiate themselves with the *Kapo* and at the same time to thank him, these Dutchmen decided to prepare a little party for him. As must be obvious, foodstuffs were scarce, but one of the Dutchmen, an illustrator by profession, found a sheet of paper from a cement bag, varnished it back and front with linseed oil to make it look like parchment, frayed its borders, traced all around it a Greek key pattern with red lead paint he had stolen on the work site, and copied onto it in beautiful calligraphy a small poem expressing good wishes. Naturally, it was in Dutch, a language I don't know, but thanks to one of memory's curious salvage operations I still remember several of its verses. Everyone signed, including Goldbaum, even though he was not Dutch but Austrian. This astonished me, but only skin-deep; then I no longer thought of it, as I too was overwhelmed by the dramatic events that followed the breakup of the *Lager* a few days later.

The name of this Goldbaum resurfaced for an instant in the course of an encounter that I describe in *The Periodic Table*. Due to an improbable twist of fate, more than twenty years later I happened to be in correspondence with a German chemist, one of my former bosses from that time: he suffered from feelings of guilt and asked me for something like forgiveness or absolution. To prove to me that he had felt human feelings for us prisoners, he cited episodes and characters, of the sort that he could have found in any of the numerous books published on the subject (or even in my own *Survival in Auschwitz**); but he also asked me for personal news about Goldbaum, whom certainly no book had mentioned. It was a small but concrete proof. I told him the little I knew: Goldbaum had died during the prisoners' terrible transfer march from Auschwitz to Buchenwald.

The name has come up again a few months ago. *The Periodic Table* was published in England, and a certain family of Bristol, but with branches in South Africa and elsewhere, wrote me a complicated letter. An uncle of theirs, Gerhard Goldbaum, had been deported, they knew not where, nor had they ever received news of him. They knew that the probabilities for an actual coincidence were minimal, be-

* See note on p. x.

cause it was a very common surname, and yet one of his nieces was prepared to come to Turin to talk to me, so as to find out if by any chance my Goldbaum was in fact their lost relation, to whose memory they seemed very attached.

Before answering, I tried to mobilize all that I remembered of Goldbaum. It wasn't much: we belonged to the same squad, ambitiously named the "Chemical Kommando," but he was not a chemist, nor had we been friends particularly. Nevertheless, I connected him with a vague reminiscence of a privileged position similar to mine: I recognized him (in truth, quite late) as belonging to some other technical specialization. His German was limpid: undoubtedly, he had been a civilized and well-cultivated man. I reread the letters from the German chemist, and in them I found a piece of information that I had forgotten: the Goldbaum he remembered had been a physicist who specialized in sound, like me he had been examined and then assigned to an acoustics laboratory.

That circumstance brought back to mind a coincidence I had forgotten: in Solzhenitsyn's *The First Circle* there are described strange, specialized *Lager*, one in particular, in which the engineer-prisoners are employed in the development of a sound analyzer "commissioned" by Stalin's secret police for the purpose of identifying human voices in telephonic interceptions. Many of these *Lager* sprang up in the Soviet Union after the end of the war. Now, in April 1945, that is, after the Liberation, I had been invited for an interview by an extremely polite Soviet official: he had learned that as a prisoner I had worked in a chemistry laboratory, and he wanted to know from me how much the Germans gave us to eat, how closely they watched us, whether they paid us, how they prevented thefts and sabotage. It is therefore quite probable that I modestly contributed to the organization of the Soviets' so-called *saraski*, and it is not impossible that Goldbaum's mysterious work was the kind described by Solzhenitsyn.

I wrote back to the Z——s that I would go to London in April: their trip to Italy was unnecessary, we would be able to see each other there. They came to the appointment, seven of them belonging to three generations, they laid siege to me, and right off they showed me two photographs of Gerhard snapped around 1939. I experienced a kind of bedazzlement; at a distance of almost half a century that was the face, it coincided perfectly with the one that I, without knowing it, bore imprinted in the pathological memory I preserve of that period: at times, but only for what concerns Auschwitz, I feel I am the brother of Ireneo Funes, *"el memorioso"* described by Borges, the man who remembered every leaf of every tree he had ever seen, and who "by himself had more memories than all the men who ever existed since the world began." No further proofs were needed: I told this to the niece, the leader of the family, but instead of slackening, their pressure increased; I don't speak in metaphors, I was supposed to meet with other people, but the Z——s had encapsulated me in the way that leukocytes surround a germ, they closed in on me and harried me with questions. I was unable to answer all the questions, save one: no, Goldbaum must not have suffered too much from hunger; that was attested to by the very fact that I had immediately recognized him in the photograph. In my mental image were absent the signs of extreme hunger, unmistakable and well known to me; his trade, until the very last days, must have saved him at least from suffering that torture.

And also the Dutch puzzle was solved. It was a further confirmation: the niece told me that at the time of Austria's annexation Gerhard had taken refuge in Holland, where by then, having learned the language, he had worked for Philips until the Nazi invasion. He belonged to the Dutch Resistance; like me, he had been arrested as a partisan, and later identified as a Jew.

The affectionate and tumultous clan of the Z——s was with difficulty dispersed by an improvised "disciplinary squad," but before leaving me the niece handed me a small package. It contained a woolen scarf: I will wear it next winter. For the time being I've put it away in a drawer, with the sensation of someone who touches an object that has fallen from the cosmos, like lunar stones, or the "materializations" boasted of by spiritualists.

August 10, 1986

T I M E   C H E C K M A T E D
. . .

GRAND DUCHY OF NEUSTRIA
CENTRAL PATENT OFFICE

Patent Application No. 861731
Class 23, Group 2
Date of request: February 2, 1984

I, Theophil Skoptza, born at Obikon, on July 31, 1919, by occupation forest ranger, submit application so that I may be granted a patent for the invention described hereinafter.

State of the Art

It is known to common experience that the step of time as it is perceived by each individual does not coincide with that indicated by so-called objective instruments. According to my measurements, one minute spent in front of a red traffic light is on the average 8 times longer than one minute spent conversing with a friend; 22 times if the friend is of the opposite sex. A commercial on the TV of this Grand

Duchy is perceived to be 5 to 10 times longer than its actual time, which rarely goes beyond one minute. One hour spent under conditions of sensory deprivation acquires erratic values that vary from a few minutes to 15 to 18 hours. A night spent in a state of insomnia is longer than a night spent sleeping, but to the best of my knowledge to this day no quantitative research has been developed. As is known to everyone, subjective time lengthens enormously if watches or chronometers are frequently consulted.

Equally common is the observation that subjective time lengthens in the course of disagreeable experiences or conditions, such as toothache or seasickness, migraine, long waits, and such. However, because of the viciousness intrinsic to the human condition and nature, it becomes short, even evanescent, in the course of the opposite conditions.

Invention

It is protected by the registered trademark PARACHRON, which includes all grammatical derivations thereof. It presupposes normal physiological conditions on the part of the subject, and it consists in the injection of extremely small doses of rubidium maleate into the fourth cerebral ventricle. The operation is neither dangerous nor painful, and to date no harmful side effects have been evident, except for a slight feeling of dizziness during the first days following the injection. After a period of latency lasting a few days, the patient is in a position to act voluntarily upon his subjective sense of time. Not only can he make it uniform with objective duration, but he can actually reverse the phenomenon, that is, lengthen the time of agreeable experiences at will and abbreviate the duration of painful or vexing experiences. In the second instance it must be pointed out that in a totally unforeseen fashion, muscular activity, memory, attention, and perception retain their integrity; this fact distinguishes the method here described from techniques such as narcosis, hypnosis, coma, or induced catalepsy, as well as from the time machines invented for the time being only by novelists.

Examples

Example 1. H.D., age 49, messenger and driver. Was forced by his profession to stand on line for hours at the Bureau of Records, which in this Grand Duchy is particularly inefficient. After parachronal treatment he reports that he sees the line in front of him growing shorter at a pace that he evaluates at 3 persons per second, to the point of having the impression that he must run in order to get to the window before missing his turn. He has grown in height, his gray hairs have returned to their original color, and he has devoted himself successfully to the Urdu language.

Example 2. L.E., age 19, student. After undergoing parachron, she no longer notices the anxiety of exams, and as a consequence is freed from a specific anguish (caused in fact by the long waiting period) that rendered her incapable of answering questions and resulted in her failing innumerable times, although she was excellently prepared and had an IQ of 148.

Example 3. T.K., age 35, lathe operator, unemployed, presently under preventive arrest, waiting for trial. He has served 35 months of detention, assessing them at 4 days. He reports that he sees daybreak as though with a jerk and nightfall with the same suddenness "after a few seconds." Despite all this, in prison he has read the complete works of Ken Follett and remembers the contents very well.

Example 4. F.P., factory worker, age 24. By her own admission, she has a difficult character, and she was angered when her fiancé came to their dates 20 or 30 minutes late. She underwent the parachron treatment, and now she does not notice the latenesses, which have become imperceptible, and their relationship has been reestablished to the satisfaction of both parties.

Example 5. T.S., age 67 (this is me). After undergoing the treatment, I happened to discover a small porcine mushroom that had just sprouted in the underbush. I immediately put myself in a parachronic mode, and I picked a mushroom weighing 0.760 kilograms after a wait of 3 days and 3 nights, which to me appeared in all no longer than half an hour. So intense was this that I saw the mushroom literally grow before my eyes.

Example 6. G.G., age 27, degree in Neustrian literature but temporarily a house painter. Treated with rubidium maleate on July 25, 1982. During the first, long-hoped-for carnal embrace with the woman he loved, at the peak of orgasm he was able to put himself instantaneously in the parachronic mode, that is, perform on himself the operation that had such bad results with Faust. He reports that he maintained the exalted condition for a time that he evaluates at 36 hours, even though his normal orgasms objectively last no longer than 5 to 7 seconds. At the end he was not only rested and lucid but full of active energy: presently he is preparing for a solitary winter climb of the south wall of the Aconcagua. He further reports that his partner, although she did not notice anything at the moment, has decided to be parachronized in my laboratory as soon as possible.

Claims

1. A method to accelerate, slow down, or arrest subjective time at the subject's will, characterized by the fact that the psychophysiological modification is obtained by means of the introduction into the organism of the organic salt of an alkaline metal.

2. A method as described in the preceding claim, characterized by the fact that the introduction takes place by means of injection into the liquid contained in the fourth cerebral ventricle.

3. A method as described in the preceding claim, characterized by the fact that the injected substance (recognized as the most active among the many tested) is rubidium maleate.

4. A method as described in the preceding claims, characterized by the fact that the quantity of active principle employed varies from 2 to 12 picograms per kilogram of the subject's body weight.

September 12, 1986

THE TOMMY-GUN
UNDER THE BED
∎ ∎ ∎

At the time of Mussolini's Republic of Salò, my sister was twenty-three years old. She was a partisan courier, and this entailed tasks that were various but always dangerous: transportation and distribution of underground printed matter, exhausting races by bicycle to maintain liaison, black market, even taking in and treating partisans who were wounded or, a frequent thing, "had reached the end of their tether." She was a good courier because she was strongly motivated: both her fiancé and I had been deported and to all effects had vanished from the face of the earth (her fiancé never did return). Her militancy not only sprang from political reasons but was both retaliation and vindication.

She had perennially to stay on the alert and often changed her place of residence: indeed, she did not have a fixed abode, she lived a bit here and a bit there, at times in Turin with friends who were not suspect, who took her in willingly or unwillingly, at times in the countryside with my mother, who also was hidden on a permanent basis. She was a girl alien to violence; yet in June 1945, that is, after the Liberation had taken place, she kept a Beretta tommy-gun under her bed. When I questioned her, she said that she no longer remembered where it came from, or for which unit it was meant; perhaps it needed some repairs, then it had simply remained there. There were many other things to worry about . . .

Now it so happened that a certain Cravero came to see her. I mentioned this episode in *The Reawakening*: Cravero was a professional thief with whom I had lived for some months at Katowice after the arrival of the Russians. He had been the first to attempt spontaneous repatriation, and he carried a letter of mine, something that was in itself good (this was the only news from me that reached Italy during the eighteen months of my absence); something not so good, he attempted to extort money "to return to Poland and look for me," and since he didn't succeed, he stole my sister's bicycle at the foot of the stairs. He got a look at that tommy-gun, which was not well hidden, and made a cautious offer that my sister wisely turned down.

After that strange visit, and after having read the letter, my sister got the idea of going to the Polish military command in Milan to ask for news about me. I must point out here that these were "Anders' Poles," that army of courageous desperados whom the Allies had salvaged from the Soviet prison camps, rearmed, and reorganized; between them and the Russians there was bad blood. Perhaps slightly allergic to our surname Levi, they received her with distrust and incredulity. If I were in the hands of the Russians I could not be in Poland, and if I were in Poland I could not be in the hands of the Russians: and in any case they themselves found it difficult to communicate with their country. My sister, who does not give up easily, was not satisfied, and two days later she went to the Soviet military command. Here she was received with a bit more cordiality but also did not succeed in accomplishing anything: the official on duty told her that if I was in Soviet hands I had nothing to fear, that in the USSR foreigners enjoyed the greatest respect, but that, alas, due to the difficulty of communicating, they were unable to put her in touch with me, even less arrange for my repatriation. She must wait and trust.

On leaving the headquarters, my sister noticed something curious. She was being tailed: the usual Italian policeman disguised as a policeman, who had followed her and then waited for her in a café across the street. Evidently, the Poles had reported my sister's "suspect" moves and contacts to the Italian police, who had gone into action immediately but amateurishly. In the euphoric and chaotic climate of the Liberation, the matter would have not been worrisome at all if it hadn't been for the tommy-gun; but in that same climate, despite Draconian laws, one did not easily give up a tommy-gun: it might still come in handy, who knows how or when or against whom. What's more, the Resistance had just barely ended, and such a weapon had a charisma that rendered it only slightly less than sacred: now, one doesn't sell, give away, or throw into the Po a sacred shield that dropped from heaven. Bundled up in a few rags, the tommy-gun therefore remained in the house until, a few days later, the maladroit shadower knocked at the door and very ceremoniously asked my sister for an interview. It was a confused interview: my sister tells me that it hinged mainly on Cravero, whom the Poles considered a liar, a provocateur, or even a Soviet spy. Out of a pure sense of duty, or a professional reflex, the policeman did not neglect to carry out a search, which, however, was confined to a quick look at the attic in which my sister lived at the time. There is no doubt that he saw the mummy of the tommy-gun, but he didn't bat an eye, and left. Maybe he was an ex-partisan: for a brief period among the detectives there were also some of them.

Along about August, not without bureaucratic pangs, my sister was allowed to regain possession of our house, which had been sequestered during the racial laws, and she took the tommy-gun along. At this point that instrument of death had become something halfway between a symbol of the Resistance's passion, an amulet, bric-a-brac, and a monument to itself. My mild sister oiled it properly and hid it in the library behind Balzac's complete works, which had approximately the same length. In fact, she forgot about it, or almost. When I, just as mild as she, returned from the prison camps in October, while looking for I don't remember what, I found it and asked about it. "Can't you see? It's a Beretta," my sister answered, with unfeigned naturalness.

The tommy-gun remained behind Balzac until 1947, the year in which Scelba became Minister of the Interior. His efficient task force began to give me some worries: if they ever found it, I as the head of the family would go to prison. The opportunity to get rid of it arose unexpectedly. Out of nowhere a partisan showed up, in fact a *"partigia,"* that is, a man belonging to the most reckless and light-fingered fringes of our fighting comrades. He was a Sicilian, and, tired of so much calm, he had set himself up as a separatist. He was looking for arms: he'd come just in time! I let him have the tommy-gun—not without some misgivings, because I did not sympathize with the Sicilian separatist movement. Neither he nor his phantasmal movement had any money. We immediately agreed on a swap: he, who would never again set foot on the Alps, gave me a pair of used mountain boots, which I have to this day.

Then the *"partigia"* vanished, but since the world is small, a few months later he was sighted by a cousin of mine who in those days lived in Brazil. He had the tommy-gun with him, for who knows what purpose; it seems that customs, so attentive to chocolates and cartons of cigarettes, is blind when faced by less innocuous objects. I would feel reassured if I were to learn that the weapon is in the hands of the Indios of the Amazon, who are desperately defending their identity: it would have remained faithful to its original vocation.

October 24, 1986

ESSAYS

A VALLEY
. . .

There is a valley that I alone know.
You do not reach it easily,
There are crags at its entrance,
Brushwood, secret fords, and swift waters,
And the paths are reduced to faint traces.
Most maps overlook it:
I found the way in by myself.
I devoted years to it,
Often, as happens, making mistakes,
But it was not wasted time.
I do not know who was there before,
One, or someone, or no one:
That is a matter of no importance.
There are marks on slabs of rock,
Some beautiful, all mysterious,
Some certainly not by human hand.
Toward the bottom there are beeches and birches;
On high, firs and larches
Ever more sparse, tormented by the wind,
Which in the spring robs them of their pollen

When the first marmots awaken.
Higher up still are seven lakes
Of uncontaminated water,
Limpid, dark, gelid, and deep.
At this level our local plants
End, but almost at the pass
There is a single, vigorous tree,
Flourishing and always green,
To which no one has yet given a name:
Perhaps it is the one of which Genesis speaks.
It bears flowers and fruit in all seasons,
Even when the snow weighs heavy on its branches.
There is no other of the same species:
It fertilizes itself.
Its trunk bears old wounds
From which a resin drips
Bitter and sweet, the bringer of oblivion.

THE COMMANDER
OF AUSCHWITZ
∎ ∎ ∎

Richard Baer, the SS major of whose arrest we have just heard, was the successor to Rudolf Höss in the position of commander of the Auschwitz concentration camp. I was his subject for almost a year, one of his hundred thousand slaves; together with another ten thousand I was in fact "rented out" by him to the I.G. Farbenindustrie, the mastodontic German chemical trust, which for each of us paid four to eight marks a day as salary for our work. Paid, but not to us: just as you don't pay a horse or an ox, so this money was handed to our masters, that is, to the SS ruling the camp.

I belonged to him, therefore: yet I would not even recognize his face. Unless it might coincide with that of the frowning, corpulent individual, his abdomen bristling with decorations, who every morning and every evening was in the habit of attending the interminable march of our squads in step with band music on the way to and from work. But they were all identical, those faces, those voices, those attitudes: all of them distorted by the same hate and the same anger, and by the lust of omnipotence. So their hierarchy was obscure to us—SS, Gestapo, Labor Services, Party, Factory, the whole enormous machine stood above us, and appeared to us flattened, without perspective: an imperium of night and fog whose structure we did not know. Until today not much was known about Richard Baer. He is briefly mentioned in the memoirs of Höss, his predecessor, who described him in the terrifying weeks of January 1945 as perplexed and uncertain as to what he should do: he is at Gross-Rosen, a *Lager* of ten to twelve thousand prisoners, and he is diligently concentrating on transferring there the forty thousand from Auschwitz, whom it is necessary to "salvage" in the face of the sudden Russian advance. Just think of what the relationship between these two figures signifies: just think about that other solution, which common sense and humanity and prudence all together suggested—that is, accepting the inevitable, leaving the throngs of half-dead to their destiny, opening the doors, and departing. Think about all this, and the sort of man we are dealing with will appear before us reasonably well defined.

He belongs to the century's most dangerous human type. If you look carefully, without him, without the Hösses, the Eichmanns, the Kesselrings, without thousands of other faithful and blind executors of orders, the great savage beasts, Hitler, Himmler, and Goebbels, would have been impotent and disarmed. Their names would not appear in history: they would have passed like grim meteors through Europe's dark sky. But the opposite happened: the seed sown by these black apostles, as history has shown, struck root in Germany with disconcerting speed and depth in all social classes and led to a proliferation of hatred that to this day poisons Europe and the world.

Resistance was timid and rare, and was immediately overwhelmed: the National Socialist message found an echo precisely in the Germans' traditional virtues, in their sense of discipline and national cohesion, their unquenched thirst for primacy, their propensity for slavish obedience.

This is why men like Baer are dangerous: men who are too loyal, too faithful, too docile. It must be taken as either heresy or sacrilege: in the spirit of the whole, upright man whom modern morality should point to as an example, there will always, despite everything, be a place for love of country and intelligent conscious obedience.

A question arises spontaneously: what should one say of the German people of today? How should one judge them? What should one expect from them?

It is difficult to auscultate the heartbeat of a people. Anyone who travels in Germany today finds the outward appearances that I found everywhere. A growing affluence, peaceful people, large and small intrigues, a moderate subversive atmosphere; on the stands, newspapers like ours, conversations like ours on trains and in trams; a few scandals that end like all scandals. And yet in the air you sense something that you do not sense elsewhere. Anyone who takes them to task for the dreadful events of recent history rarely finds repentance, or even critical consciousness: much more often he encounters an ambiguous response, in which are intertwined a feeling of guilt, a desire for vindication, and a deliberate and impudent ignorance.

Therefore, the so strangely slow and tortuous behavior of the German police and magistrature should not astonish. The picture is confused and rich in contradictions, but a substantially defined line of conduct seems to emerge from it: for its past actions, the slaughters and sufferings inflicted on Europe, Germany intends, so to speak, to be responsible civilly, not penally. It is known that the German government has publically shown itself ready to grant monetary indemnification to the victims of Nazism in all the countries previously occupied (but not in Italy), and the same has been done or is being done by a number of German industries that exploited slave labor during the war. But police and magistrature have proven much less ready to complete the purges initiated by the Allies: so we have reached today's disconcerting situation, in which it can happen that a commander of Auschwitz lives and works undisturbed in Germany for fifteen years, and that the executioner of millions of innocents is tracked down, not indeed by the German police but "illegally" by victims who slipped through his hands.

December 23, 1960

THE MOON AND MAN*
▪ ▪ ▪

They are on their way back, and they are well. How can we define their exploit? Even our lexicon has become inadequate: to call it a "flight," "cavalcade," or "navigation" would amount to diminishing it and depriving it of color—they would be reverse hyperbole. Now it is up to us, to all of us spectators (and also, as such, to some degree actors), to think about it and draw conclusions.

It seems that in a few days common consciousness has changed, as always happens after a qualitative leap: you tend to forget the cost, the effort, the risks and sacrifices. They were there undoubtedly, and they were enormous: nevertheless, today we still ask ourselves whether it was "money well spent." We can see it today, and yesterday we could see it less well: the enterprise was not to be judged on a utilitarian scale, or not chiefly in those terms. In the same way, an inquiry into the costs encountered in building the Parthenon would seem jarringly out of place; it is typical of

* Published on the occasion of the flight of the three astronauts Borman, Lovell, and Anders on *Apollo 8*.

man to act in an inspired and complex manner, perhaps adding up the costs beforehand, but not confining himself to the pure, imminent, or distant advantage, to take off for remote goals, with aims that are justification in themselves: to act in order to challenge a secret, enlarge his frontiers, express himself, test himself.

Our world, in so many of its aspects sinister, provisional, diseased, and tragic, has also this other face: it is a "brave new world" that does not recoil before obstacles and does not find peace until it has circumvented, penetrated, or overwhelmed them. It is braveness of a new type: not that of the pioneer, the hero at war, the lone navigator. This, even though praiseworthy, is not very new or very rare: you can find it in all countries and in all ages, and it isn't even specifically human. Also the wolf, also the tiger and bull are brave, and so without a doubt were our distant progenitors and the Homeric heroes.

We are at once similar and different: the bravery from which the lunar adventure sprang is different, it is Copernican, it is Machiavellian. It defies other obstacles, other dangers, less bloody but longer and heavier; it confronts other enemies, it confronts common sense, it confronts the "it's always been done like this," the laziness and weariness in ourselves and around us. It fights with different arms, portentously complex and subtle, all or almost all created from nothing during the last ten or twenty years by virtue of intelligence and patience: new technologies, new substances, new energies, and new ideas. This is no longer a daring to challenge the unforeseen, but a daring to foresee everything—a quality even more courageous.

Confronted by this latest evidence of bravery and ingenuity, we can feel not only admiration and detached solidarity: in some way and with some justification each of us feels he is a participant. Just as every person, even the most innocent, even the victim himself, feels some responsibility for Hiroshima, Dallas, and Vietnam, and is ashamed, so even the one least connected with the colossal labor of cosmic flights feels that a small particle of merit falls to the human species, and so also to himself, and because of this feels that he has greater value. For good or evil, we are a single people: the more we become conscious of this, the less difficult and long will be humanity's progress toward justice and peace.

■ ■ ■

Man's survival in space is due in good part, but only in part, to the conditioned microenvironment that is accurately maintained inside the capsule: to everyone's astonishment, the astronauts have endured, without harm, the exposure to extrahuman, extraterrestrial agents that are hostile to life and that cannot be reproduced (or only imperfectly) on the planet's surface.

Man, the naked ape, the terrestrial animal who is the son of a very long dynasty of terrestrial or marine beings, molded in all of his organs by a restricted environment which is the lower atmosphere, can detach himself from it without dying. He can endure exposure to cosmic radiation, even without the domestic screen of air; he can remove himself from the familiar alternation of day and night; he can tolerate accelerations that are multiples of gravity's; he can eat, sleep, work, and think even at zero gravity—and perhaps this is the most astounding revelation, the one about which, before Gagarin's exploit, it was permissible to entertain the greatest doubts.

The human substance (or better the animal substance), besides being adaptable evolutionarily, on the scale of millions of years and at the expense of the incalculable sacrifice of the less fit variants, is adaptable today and now, on the scale of days and hours: on the screen all of us have seen the astronauts glide through space like fish in water, learn new balances and new reflexes never realized or realizable on the ground.

Therefore, not only is man strong because he has made himself so since the time a million years ago when, from among the many weapons that nature offered the animals, he opted for the brain—man is strong in himself, he is stronger than he estimated, he is made of a substance fragile only in appearance, he has been mysteriously planned with enormous, unsuspected margins of safety. We are singular animals, solid and ductile, driven by atavisitic impulses, and by reason, and at the same time by a "cheerful strength," so that, if an enterprise can be accomplished, be it good or evil, it cannot be set aside but must be carried through.

This moon flight is an initial test; other exploits await us, deeds of courage and ingenuity, much more demanding because necessary to our very survival: exploits against hunger, poverty, and suffering. These too must be felt as challenges to our valor, and these too, since they can, must be carried through.

December 27, 1968

S I C !
∎ ∎ ∎

The eclipse of the principle of authority must be counted among the few positive elements of our time: today it would not cross anyone's mind to reinforce one's statement by having recourse to quotations drawn from Latin or Greek classics, as Montaigne used to do, though he was an open spirit, critical and sensible. And yet what a subtle pleasure one can still experience when one can get his hands on an elegant and rare quotation!

Where does this pleasure come from? Sometimes it is sincere enjoyment at finding oneself so completely in agreement with a great author as to be able to insert a shred of him in one's own fabric, without this insertion showing irritation around the edges of the transplant or reactions of rejection. But more often it is a less noble pleasure; it is like saying to the reader, "You see, I draw from sources that you do not know, I know something that you do not know, and so I stand a grade higher than you."

The drive to quote is so strong that some writers quote unconsciously, in the same way that somnambulists walk: when they reread what they have written, perhaps some years later, they find in it the elected passage that rose from the depths of consciousness to the page without the intervention of will. Almost complementary is the phenomenon of the invented quotation: Rabelais, Borges, and Wilcock are masters at recording admirable sentences drawn from nonexistent books by nonexistent (or even existent) authors.

When polemicizing, it is known what base things one can perpetrate, often with impunity, quoting the adversary text in an incomplete or inexact manner. One can obtain striking effects by omitting a sentence or stitching together two sentences that were separate; the peak then is reached and a decisive score is toted up when one manages to insert in the body of the quotation a pair of brackets and write inside them: *Sic*!

This *sic* is the equivalent of a checkmate in chess or the drop shot close to the net in tennis: like these it is ruthless, and just like these it presupposes an error on the contender's part. It may be a venial error, a grammtical or even orthographic oversight, but the *sic*, this hiccup of virtuous and scandalized astonishment, blows it out of all proportion, shines upon it a light without shadows, brings it to the center of the reader's attention. SIC: the man whom I quote and from whom I obviously dissent as every decent person must dissent, is, my dear sirs, a dunce. He dares to write in our language but does not know it, so that he ends up by putting on paper enormities such as this. Yes, *sic*, that's precisely what he says, go ahead and compare it with the original. How can you trust him? He has put the subject in the objective case: thus every one of his statements is suspect, and every one of his opinions must be handled with tongs.

March 13, 1977

OUR DREAMS
■ ■ ■

In his *Galateo*, Monsignor Della Casa insistently recommends that one mustn't "recite" one's dreams. Della Casa had not read Freud, and so he did not worry about the greater danger the dreamer may run, that of unknowingly divulging his most jealous secrets; but he was a man of good sense and good taste, and he had observed what everybody sooner or later observes, that is, that our dreams can be heavy with significance or at least emotion for us but are always pure boring nonsense for our interlocutor. So anyone who "recites" them is no less a nuisance to his listeners than, for example, the person who boasts of his aristocratic lineage, or who simply makes a great noise when he blows his nose.

One can only agree with Della Casa: the dreams of others are confused and boring. If one rereads Freud's *Interpretation of Dreams*, one cannot escape the comparison between the dreams chosen by him as examples, which true enough are entangled and illogical but at the same time coruscating and greatly suggestive, and the flat stupidity of the dreams, ours and others', of which we have direct experience.

It may be that in one century, like everything else around us, the world of dreams has also changed: just as Charcot's *grande hystérie* has vanished, just as the swoons and fainting spells that studded nineteenth-century novels have disappeared, perhaps even the style of dreams may have changed. Or perhaps Freud, like all anthologists, may have (consciously or not) selected particularly significant dreams or dreams peculiarly apt to confirm his theses. But on the basis of what has recently been published on the subject, one might think of a different interpretation.

From the great cauldron of studies in so-called parapsychological phenomena a single effect seems to emerge as accessible to methodical experimentation, because, as is claimed, it is vaguely reproducible under controlled conditions—that is, the direct (without sensorial mediation) transmission of images from a waking experimenter to a sleeping subject, who receives them in the form of dreams.

These studies are mentioned by Cavanna in *Aspetti scientifici della parapsicologia* (Scientific Aspects of Parapsychology [Turin, 1973]). There is no doubt that, for the moment, they must be received with a considerable degree of skepticism, but, as is known, there are many unsuspected things between earth and heaven; and in any case, nothing prevents us right now from being amused by the thought that, despite the orthodox Freudians, our dreams are not always ours; that their violence, obscenity, and ferocity are not the tracks of monsters buried in our depths but rather the monsters of others; that their stupidity is the echo of the background noise produced by the stupidity around us; and that one might in fact get to the point, if necessary through patient training, of being able to harness the phenomenon, and so make the gift of "sweet dreams" to those who are dear to us and, conversely, inflict repugnant night-mares on our enemies: all of this at no cost and without risk.

But is it actually necessary to turn to telepathy? The siege of violence and turpitude exists and hems us in more and more. Anyone without good defenses is today already infected by it, and not only in dreams.

April 24, 1977

THE STRUGGLE
FOR LIFE
. . .

On an unforgettable page of *The Conquest of Happiness*, Bertrand Russell reminds us that the animal man, like the other animals, has in his biological makeup a certain instinct to compete, that is, to engage in the struggle for life; that therefore anyone rich or powerful enough to satisfy all of his desires without effort is deprived of a fundamental ingredient of happiness; that therefore you cannot be happy if you are not deprived of at least some of the things that you desire!

To this paradox one might add that anyone who in his own life has had the chance to verify these statements must be counted, even if not among the happy, at least among the fortunate, because if the desires whose satisfaction we must renounce become too many, or if they are numbered among the vital needs, then it is no longer a matter of happiness. The unhappiness that derives from excessive satisfaction and from lack of the struggle for life is, everything considered, quite rare, and in fact Russell himself defines it as "Byronic unhappiness" to distinguish it from others more common and more concrete, which are of the opposite sign.

We might likewise observe that while it is disagreeable to be judged, and it is humiliating and debilitating to be continually *sub judice*, to expect to elude all judgment is unnatural and dangerous. It is certainly difficult to establish case by case which judges can be accepted and which "recused," but to recuse all judges is not only presumptuous but useless. Useless because every turn in life, every human encounter, involves a judgment delivered or received, so it is a good idea to get used to receiving and delivering judgments when one is young, when it is easier to contract habits.

In the absence of such training—and it is difficult to see why it should not coincide with regular schooling and with the vaccination of the judgments received in school, in the guise of grades or any other form; it does not matter— the first negative judgment one will receive in life can be perceived as a deep wound, or can attack with the violence of a germ. Now, such a negative judgment is inevitable, because in life one comes face to face with facts, and facts are obstinate and pitiless judges.

One must be cautious in accepting an external judgment, but must nevertheless accept at least one: this cannot be avoided, since nobody can judge himself (anyone who does so, consciously or not, merely reproduces the external judgment that emotionally appears the most correct, whether positive or negative), and since living without one's actions being judged means renouncing a retrospective insight that is precious, thus exposing oneself and one's neighbor to serious risks: it is the same as piloting a boat without a compass, or wanting to maintain a constant temperature without consulting a thermometer.

For this reason, while it is right to rebel against a scholastic selection based (in fact if not in name) on wealth or social status, and against a scholastic system based exclusively on selection, it seems to me a mistake to demand a school that does not foster the habit of receiving judgments. This would perhaps be a charitable or welfare institution, but only over the short term: I do not believe that it would produce truly free and responsible citizens.

July 3, 1977

S P E A R S   B E C O M E
S H I E L D S
∎ ∎ ∎

Recently, a short, strange book has just been published in Italy. It is entitled *Badenheim 1939*, and it was written in 1975 by Aharon Appelfeld, an Israeli writer. It describes the season at an imaginary spa whose guests, Jews, eat *petits fours*, play tennis, gossip and do a little mild backbiting, and interlace flirtations, while an undefined "Office of Hygiene" is registering them, encircling the small town with barbed wire, and in the end will deport them all to Poland.

The book is horrifying, and can be read in many ways. Two of them stand out: as an evocation of the detachment and the "I don't want to know about it" attitude with which a past generation opposed the Hitlerian threat, and as an allusion to our obtuseness, our refusal today to acknowledge the atomic threat.

Today we too, like yesterday's foolish Jews of Badenheim, eat *petits fours* and organize music festivals while the Office of Hygiene is at work; but today's situation is different. The threat concerns no longer only a minority but in fact the human species; it no longer emanates from a single and perverse center of power but is intrinsic to the precarious balance in which we have become accustomed to living.

One willingly talks about apocalypses and scourges when they seem distant, perhaps even jokes about them, as in *Dr. Strangelove*: it was amusing, but today we would see it again with some discomfort. When, on the other hand, their step approaches, we behave as they did in Badenheim. The fact that today one speaks about them, gives lectures and holds round-table discussions, that demonstrations take place everywhere is a moderately positive sign: it means we believe, rightly or wrongly, that our fate has not been sealed, that there still is a bit of time, and that discussion is useful.

It is, of course, useful to discuss it in the international forums; but it is also useful to discuss it in the living room, around a table at the bar, among friends and strangers. It is an opportunity to turn one's back on the childish rhetoric of rabid patriotism and to grapple with a concrete problem.

I believe that first of all we must make an effort to be impartial, say it and prove that we are, even if this is not easy. When we descend into the streets and shout that we want to impose atomic disarmament on our governments, we must be very clear: we are addressing all governments, and we fear all nuclear warheads. There aren't some good and some bad—they're all bad.

It's not easy to be impartial, because when it comes to "imposing" and "addressing" there is no symmetry between the two halves of the world. To organize a demonstration in Rome or New York, all that is needed is an agreement between people who think in the same way; to organize it in Moscow, the agreement of Moscow is needed. The day we shall hear that in Moscow there has been a spontaneous peaceful demonstration will be a great day for all of humanity. This day does not seem very close, but convincing the Russians that our demonstrations are spontaneous and our pacifism is impartial can contribute much to bringing it closer. The East-West borders have a great capacity to absorb sounds, but if we shall have enough voice, maybe an echo of it will reach even over there and persuade those citizens (who are not all of them automatons, nor all of them deaf) to ask their government for what we ask of ours.

I believe that a certain amount of optimism is required, without which one doesn't accomplish anything and one lives badly. "There's no longer anything to be done" is an intrinsically suspect statement and of no practical utility; it serves only as an exorcism for him who utters it; that is, it isn't of much use. I don't mean to say by this that nuclear holocaust is impossible: the forty thousand bombs ready to be used do, unfortunately, exist, almost all of them stored in the United States and the Soviet Union. They are a dangling sword, but there is still something one can do, the sentence has not yet been pronounced.

As long as the fate of the world will be decided by astute and cynical but cautious old men, as until now Brezhnev and Reagan have shown themselves to be, the bombs will probably remain in their silos. In the teeth of Marxist and Tolstoyan historiography it really does seem that the masses today carry very little weight. And that in the White House or in the Kremlin sits one man rather than another makes a difference: these powerful men decide on their own, and our fates are decided by, all told, less than three thousand grams of cerebral matter.

Before deciding, however, they listen to advice, sniff the air, weigh internal and external desires and threats. They are not impervious to pressure from below. Leaving all moral judgments aside, we would be satisfied if they possessed two qualities: that they knew how to make rational decisions, and that they had complete control over their subordinates, especially the military. As long as this is so, they will not push the button, nor will they allow it to be pushed, because they know that the holocaust will overwhelm even their power and their lives; and they will keep at bay irresponsible and emotional allies within their borders as well as in third countries. In this connection it is incomprehensible, criminal, and suicidal to allow governments (including ours!) to supply unstable countries with potentially death-dealing materials and technologies.

Finally, I believe that realism is needed. To ask for everything now and immediately is naïve, and extremist slogans are stillborn. It is right to exhort that spears be converted into ploughshares, Isaiah already did so; but we must remember that the makers of "spears" are powerful and dogged. It would be wonderful to force them to change trades, but we would not be able to do this in a short time. Staying with the image, I propose that the conversion should be gradual; spears into shields, and then shields into ploughshares, when prudence permits.

In short, would it not be possible to invest the dizzying amounts of money allotted to the military budgets mainly (and gradually) in defensive weapons? In radar networks instead of nuclear warheads, in antitank missiles instead of tanks, and so on? This would be an unequivocal signal to the opposite camp that the guard has not been lowered but that there are no aggressive intentions.

America and Russia find themselves in a costly stalemate in which, for reasons of long distrust and also barbaric prestige, no one wants to take the first step on the path of disarmament. This would be a first step acceptable also to someone who still responds to the fascination of weapons. If this were put into effect, the world's safety would take a step forward, small but sure.

This is simply the proposal of an incompetent: candid, presumptuous, or even ridiculous, but it is a proposal, it is neither an exclamation nor the usual refrain nor a disconsolate sigh. Anyone who considers it absurd must counter it with another proposal; this ought to be the rule of the game, and it is a game whose stakes are very high indeed.

It appears that soon there will begin in Geneva a global negotiation: we small men find ourselves forced to delegate to two great men a responsibility more onerous than any ever before. We would like them to hear the hum of our voices and to remember that the problem of nuclear disarmament is problem number one; if it is solved, all other problems on the planet will not be automatically solved, but if it is not solved, no other problem will be solved.

November 4, 1981

TRANSLATING KAFKA
⋅ ⋅ ⋅

The comments that followed my translation of Kafka's novel *The Trial* have induced me to change my mind about quite a number of matters, both as to the line I followed in my rendition of the text and as to the motives that compelled me to declare in plain print that "I don't think I have much affinity for Kafka." If this is so, why did I choose or accept to translate him? Let us see.

Translating a book is not like contracting a matrimony or becoming a partner in a business. We can feel attracted even to someone who is very different from us, precisely because he is: if it were not so, writers, readers, and translators would become stratified in castes as rigid as in the Indian system, there would be no transverbal links nor cross-fertilization, and everyone would read only the writers who are related to him, the world would be (or appear to be) less varied, and new ideas would no longer be born.

Now, I love and admire Kafka because he writes in a way that is totally unavailable to me. In my writing, for good or evil, knowingly or not, I've always strived to pass from the darkness into the light, as (I think that Pirandello also said this, I don't remember where) a filtering pump might do, which sucks up turbid water and expels it decanted: possibly sterile. Kafka forges his path in the opposite direction: he endlessly unravels the hallucinations that he draws from incredibly profound layers, and he never filters them. The reader feels them swarm with germs and spores: they are gravid with burning significances, but he never receives any help in tearing through the veil or circumventing it to go and see what it conceals. Kafka never touches ground, he never condescends to giving you the end of Ariadne's thread.

But this love of mine is ambivalent, close to fear and rejection: it is similar to the emotion we feel for someone dear who suffers and asks us for help we cannot give. I do not much believe in the laughter of which Brod speaks: perhaps Kafka laughed when he told stories to his friends, sitting at a table in the beer hall, because one isn't always equal to oneself, but he certainly didn't laugh while he wrote. His suffering is genuine and continuous, it assails you and does not let you go: you feel like one of his characters, condemned by an abject and inscrutable, tentacular tribunal that invades the city and the world, nestling in filthy attics but also in the dark solemnity of the cathedral; or transformed into a clumsy and cumbersome insect, disliked by all, desperately alone, obtuse, incapable of communicating or thinking, capable at this point only of suffering.

Kafka understands the world (his, and even better ours of today) with a clairvoyance that astonishes and wounds like a too intense light: often one is tempted to interpose a screen, to protect oneself; at times one yields to the temptation of looking at him fixedly, and then one is blinded. And just as, when one stares at the sun's disk and then continues to see it for a long time, superimposed on the objects that surround us, so, after having read this *Trial*, we suddenly realize that we're surrounded, besieged by witless, iniquitous, and often lethal trials.

The trial brought against the diligent and narrow-minded bank official concludes in fact with a death sentence, never pronounced, never written; and the execution takes place in the most squalid, denuded environment, without pomp and without anger, with bureaucratic meticulousness, at the hands of two puppet-executioners, who fulfill their task mechanically, without saying a word, trading silly compliments. It is a page that takes your breath away. I, a survivor of Auschwitz, would never have written it, or never in that way: out of inability, or insufficient imagination, certainly, but also out of a feeling of shame before death that Kafka did not know, or, if he did, rejected; or perhaps out of lack of courage.

The famous and most commented sentence that closes the book like a tombstone (". . . it was as if the shame of it must outlive him") does not seem at all enigmatic to me. Of what should Joseph K. be ashamed, the very man who had decided to fight until death, and who at every turn in the book proclaims himself innocent? He is ashamed of many contradictory things, because he is incoherent, and his essence (like that of almost all of us) consists of being incoherent, not equal to himself during the course of time, unstable, erratic, or even divided at the same instant, split in two or more personalities that do not jibe.

He is ashamed of having struggled with the tribunal of the cathedral, and at the same time of not having resisted with sufficient energy the tribunal in the attics. Of having wasted his life in petty office jealousies, false loves, sick timidities, static and obsessive tasks. Of existing when by now he should no longer exist: of not having found the strength to do away with himself when all was lost, before the two clownish bearers of death called on him. But in this shame I sense another component that I know: Joseph K., at the end of his anguished journey, experiences shame because there exists this occult, corrupt tribunal that pervades everything surrounding him, and to which belong even the prison chaplain and the precociously lewd little girls who importune the painter Titorelli. It is in the end a human, not a divine, tribunal: it is composed of men and made by men, and Joseph K. with the knife already planted in his heart is ashamed of being a man.

June 5, 1983

RHYMING ON THE COUNTERATTACK
■ ■ ■

Anyone who has ever had contact with the world of printed paper knows how large the supply of poetry is today (but not only today) and by comparison how scant is the demand. It follows, as with any merchandise, that poetry is devalued; those who compete for the albeit very numerous prizes can be counted by the hundreds, even when the prize is purely symbolic: perhaps only a medal or a sheepskin.

The reasons for this oversupply are manifold. In the front line, and fundamentally, is the need to make poetry, which is of all countries and all times. Poetry lives within us, like music and song. There is not a civilization that is without it; it is undoubtedly more ancient than prose, if by poetry one means any discourse, verbal or written, in which the voice rises in tone, the expressive tension is great, and just as great is the attention paid to the sign and its density. In order to obtain this result, all "poetics" have elaborated a code of their own; the codes are different from one another, but they all have in common a system of signals capable of warning the reader, "Listen carefully, I am not talking idly: my discourse, even though subdued, intends to be heard and remembered." In passing, this should be said: it is significant that the codes are almost always formulated after the fact, that is, when a particular form of poetics has already borne fruit. For that matter, the same thing happens with all codes, including those properly so called, that ratify and carve on bronze or stone names and prohibitions that already existed before. One doesn't know who invented the octave or the sonnet; one knows who codified them. The legislator of poetry is not the poet but the grammarian. Indeed, the poet tends to violate the norm: at times he transgresses it due to incompetence, at other times because he feels it is too narrow for him, at still others due to a conscious will to violate it. Thus, he goes back over the path that the poetics of the moment had traveled, instituting violations of the plain language. Since poetry is intrinsic violence done to everyday language, it is understandable that every true poet feels the drive to become a violator, that is, an innovator, in his own right: to invent his own poetics, which stands in relation to the reigning poetics as the latter stands to prose.

This is the reason why making poetry is not taught in school: the same reason why neither speaking nor walking is taught. These are all activities to which we are predisposed genetically, and which we learn to perform with ease and pleasure, even if not spontaneously. We do not need study, we need (and it is enough) the example; setting out from which, each one of us develops that personal style which informs his speech, his step, and his verse. Just as we speak and walk, we are all of us, at least potentially, poets. To make poetry is to innovate, and innovating cannot be taught.

Another reason for the oversupply of poetry is to be found in the upheaval that poetic technique has undergone since the beginning of this century, since the moment, in fact, when the crisis of civilization and the decline of the

West were first spoken of. Not by chance, parallel earth-quakes have thrown into confusion music, psychology, phys-ics, linguistics, economics—in short, our whole way of life. In appearance (but only in appearance) the European poetry of our century has thrown off all shackles. After centuries of almost undisputed authority, classical metrics and prosody have faded away. Nobody has unseated them officially, but there is no doubt that in the common perception they seem obsolete, or even afflicted by a negative sign. Anyone who today were to write a sonnet conforming to the canonic rules would be considered unequipped, a survivor, or a parodist.

This apparent freedom has flung open the doors to the army of born poets: and, as said before, all of us are born poets. From these two sources, the need for singing and incantation that all of us have and the falling away of formal shackles, comes the flood of poetic books. It is a harmful phenomenon because it threatens to distract attention from the authentic new voices that certainly exist scattered among the crowd.

For this reason, but not only because of it, I hope for a spontaneous return (this is not a paradox) of the norm, in particular that of rhyme; indeed, I foresee it at hand, because in all human affairs there are retroactions that correct de-viations. Rhyme is rather a late but "probable" invention: I mean to say, it is one of those inventions that are in the air and then materialize in various places. In fact, we find it in poetic traditions very distant from one another in time and space. Its eclipse today in Western poetry seems to me inexplicable, and it is certainly temporary.

It has too many virtues, it is too beautiful to disappear. It discreetly marks the end of the verse or stanza, it rees-tablishes the ancient kinship between poetry and music, the two daughters of our need for rhythm: there are those who maintain that we acquire it before birth by listening to the beat of the maternal heart, so that we are all poets in the womb. It underlines the key words, those to which the reader's attention should be attracted. But I would like to insist on two further advantages of rhyme, one in favor of the reader of verse, the other in favor of the writer.

Whoever reads good verses wants to take them along with him, remember them, possess them. Often he does not even need to study them: things unfold as though the recording took place spontaneously, naturally, without pain (whereas the recording of texts in which we do not perceive beauty is painful or at least laborious). Now, for recording by memory, rhyme is a fundamental help: one verse line pulls along another or the others, the forgotten verse can be reconstructed, at least approximately. The effect is so strong that, in the mysterious but limited storehouse of our memory, poetry without rhyme often makes room for rhymed poetry, even if the latter is not as noble. From this follows a pragmatic consequence: poets who wish to be remembered (in Italian *ricordati*, "carried in the heart": and in many languages, memorizing is called learning "by heart") should not neglect this virtue of rhyme.

The other virtue is more subtle. Anyone who sets out to compose in rhyme imposes on himself a limitation, which, however, is rewarding. He is committed to ending a verse not with the word dictated by discursive logic but with another, stranger word, which must be drawn from the few that end "in the right way." And so he is compelled to deviate, to leave the path that is easier because it is predictable; now, reading what is predictable bores us and so does not inform us. The restriction of rhyme obliges the poet to resort to the unpredictable: compels him to invent, to "find"; and to enrich his lexicon with unusual terms; bend his syntax; in short, innovate. His situation is similar to that of the mason who agrees to use irregular bricks, polyhedral or prismatic, mixed in with the normal ones; his building will be less smooth, less functional, perhaps also less solid, but it will say more to the imagination of anyone who looks at it, and it will bear the mark of the one who built it.

Therefore, rhyme, and the rules in general, also acquire the function of revealing the writer's personality; and indeed we notice that the reciprocal distances are greater between poets than between writers of prose. The attribution of a poem is easier than that of a piece of prose. Confronted by the metric obstacle, the author is forced (forces himself) to execute a leap that is acrobatic and whose style is strictly his own: he signs every verse whether he wants it, knows it, or not.

March 26, 1985

DEAR HORACE
■ ■ ■

Dear Horace:

I've made up my mind to write to you now, that is, a few years before the bimillennial of your death, in order to get to you before my more authorized competitors, that is, the accredited experts, as one says nowadays: in any case, choral celebrations, at a set date, probably never pleased you either. Moreover, the idea came to me (or returned to me) while reading with great effort but much amusement one of your satires: the one in which you meet a pest in search of a recommendation on the Via Sacra and try vainly to get rid of him, until a providential occurrence saves you.

You have my congratulations: as you foresaw, you have not died completely. Your verses, as you can see, are studied and are still remembered; indeed, some have become proverbial and are quoted by people who never studied Latin. In fact, we by now speak a very corrupt Latin, and if we wish to understand the Latin of your times, which we call the times of "golden Latinity," we must study it. Nevertheless, your *carpe diem*, for example, has never been so fashionable as it is today; and Signor Fumagalli, a fine contemporary of ours, a retired librarian who has devoted his life to collecting famous sayings, reserves for you second place among the coiners of quotations, right behind a certain Dante Alighieri, about whom I will tell you on another occasion. In short, that monument "more lasting than bronze" that you patiently built still stands, even though it's eroded by time and by our vapors, and even if few tourist guides mention it.

With great effort, as I was saying: and I'm ashamed of it, because I studied Latin for a good eight years, with diligence, good teachers, and fair marks. I'm certain that it will be less arduous for you to read this letter of mine than it was for me to decipher your verses. As you can see from my writing, we neo-Latins have taken many liberties. We have slaughtered declensions and cases, except for the Romanians, I mean to say the Dacians, who have salvaged some traces of them; strange, isn't it? But they've always been a strange people. And besides, yes, Latins, but in the meantime we've had so many people of all races underfoot, and they have, after all, left their marks: and not only on the language.

Let us for the moment leave aside questions of linguistics: in the meantime—I cannot keep this from you—many things have happened. The Roman Empire grew immeasurably, and then it fell apart. A Judean, born a few years after your death, preached important things and made a clean sweep of the gods of Olympus, who in any case were not all that close to your heart. Now, almost throughout the world, people worship only one god, but customs have not improved because of this. We have, at least theoretically, abolished slavery. From the Alps and the sea have come Germans, Huns, and Arabs; they're brought with them plagues and wars but also new laws, and they've put a check on our pride.

There have been plenty of wars: in all centuries and everywhere, and since we've become ingenious we've invented increasingly ingenious weapons. The most recent, I mention in passing, would have startled Lucretius: and if, instead of leaving atoms whole, as is in the nature of things, one splits or condenses them in a certain way, one can make the world explode and kill every single man a hundred times over. Precisely during these years we are trying to disinvent this invention, which comes from the infernal regions. But this is nothing new; it seems to me it already happened in your time. The most mischievous inventors are those who build war machines, and war is what gives birth to the most mischievous inventions.

The world is round, you already suspected this; but it happens that we went to see whether it was really true. It was, and on the roads of the sea we met a new land, larger than Europe and Africa put together. We called it America, quickly massacred its inhabitants, who in any case ran around naked, and transformed it into a colony. Now, however, the colonists have become so rich and powerful that they in turn are colonizing us: their language is very much in vogue, and whoever does not understand it is in trouble. It seems to me that something of the kind happened with Greece in your day. Isn't that so?

Other things have also happened. We have a way of building ships that sail without wind or oars, machines that fly with hundreds upon hundreds of pilgrims inside, carts that run without horses. Actually, if you could see the Rome of today you would find it invaded by these carts: they are fast, but they make noise, stink, take up room, and every so often knock down a pedestrian. In short, it is a very different city. That Via Sacra of your satire is still there, amid the ruins of the Forums, but it is located a good three meters (one meter, forgive me, is three feet) below street level. As a matter of fact, what with broken bricks, rubble, and asphalt in all of our cities, the streets rise by at least a foot every century. For the moment the carts I mentioned are not allowed to travel along it: it is frequented only by idlers, whom we call tourists, and a few scholars. They come from afar, from America, Britannia, Scandia, and even from certain islands to the east of the Seri, whose every existence was unknown in your time. They carry with them a small machine that paints images as a painter might do, but smaller and more quickly.

We have other *mirabilia*. We navigate beneath the sea. There isn't a mountain that we haven't scaled. We know how to produce lightning and yoke it to our wheels. We can see the atoms, the frontiers of the universe, the inside of our abdomen. We have sent explorers to the Moon. We can *futuere* (today we use a somewhat different verb, but if I were to write it here in all four letters, perhaps the newspaper would not accept my piece) without impregnating. We know how to heal old diseases, though we have unleashed new ones. We have new poisons that procure ecstasy.

But you will be glad to hear that pests and recommendation hunters are still numerous and that your Venosa still exists, even though invaded by the above-mentioned carts, and though the greater part of Venosa's inhabitants live in America. Recently we have even rediscovered (in truth, in a rather run-down condition) your villa in Sabina, the one that was in your prayers: come now, it isn't as modest as you describe it; today we would call it a second home, and we would make you pay taxes that you would find it difficult to cover out of your author's royalties, or to obtain from Maecenas. You could have a telephone installed (you know Greek well, so an explanation of the term would be superfluous) and perhaps speak every evening with your friends in Rome and Mantua; but you would be disturbed by the railroad that passes nearby there, and by the motorcycles ("motorcycle" is another kind of cart) of the neighborhood youths. In our world, silence has become a rare and costly commodity.

Nor did the changing cycle of the seasons change. We are still cheered by spring, which drives away the snow and brings back grass to the meadows, as you said in your time with your usual elegance; our heart still contracts at the approach of autumn and then winter, which every year reminds us of each person's winter, the definitive one. Our life is longer than yours, but it is neither gayer nor more secure, nor do we have the certainty that the gods will grant a tomorrow to our yesterdays. We too shall join our father Aeneas, Tullus, Ancus, and you in the realm of shadows; we too, so insolent, so self-assured, will return to dust and shadow.

April 14, 1985

BACTERIA ROULETTE
■ ■ ■

Reading the autobiography of Salvador Luria, a native of
Turin, Nobel Prize 1969 in medicine, has involved me so
much as to induce me to overcome the reticence that derives
from my incompetence. Luria is a geneticist, that is, a man
who studies those very long talking molecules on which are
written our identity (and, to a great extent, our destiny); my
by now distant past as an organic chemist has led me to
frequent other long molecules, the mute and brute (because
desperately monotonous) molecules of synthetic poly-
mers—they have practical virtues, but they "say" nothing,
or rather, they repeat the same message to infinity. The
former stands to the latter as a novel would stand to a hy-
pothetical book that repeats from first page to last always
and only the same syllable.

This autobiography, recently published by Boringhieri
as *Storie di geni e di mi* (Stories about Geniuses and about
Myself), has in its original American edition a different title—*A Slot Machine, a Broken Test Tube: An Autobiography*.
This seems to me more eloquent than the Italian title be-

cause it hints at two of the book's fundamental themes; and actually, more generally, to two typical features of scientific research. Contrary to current opinion, which favors teamwork and the help of computers, today as yesterday the individual's commitment and intuition have a determining impact on the result: and in any case, if this were not so, what point would there be in continuing with Nobel Prizes? On this subject Luria has neither doubts nor false modesty, and in presenting his victories he does not hesitate to say "I."

On a higher level than the imposing scientific and technological institutes, or perhaps in spite of them, the brain of the lonely scientist, the "adventurer" isolated in his study or laboratory, remains the preferred instrument, without which all that is done is routine. True innovation does not come from the group, it is the fruit of reason, and reason is individual. However, research does not stand completely within the confines of pure rationality: it is necessary but amply insufficient; reason needs external nourishment, stimuli, which can come from the least predictable sources. This is the allusion contained in the money-eating machine, the slot machine* of the American title.

Luria tells us that by chance he watched a colleague (he is not a gambler himself!) who was playing one of those machines in which you insert a coin and which, not really haphazardly (because they are astutely programmed to insure earnings for the machine), sometimes return to a player a little more than the stake, often nothing, very rarely a considerable sum. This was for him the unforeseen stimulus: he sensed "that the sequence of a slot machine's winnings had something to teach someone working with bacteria."

* English in the original. —Trans.

I confess that for me, a layman, the text that follows did not clarify the analogy, or should we say, the symbol; but the moral is clear. To the researcher (and who is not a researcher?) the world presents itself as a vast tangle of symbols: it is up to him to hit on their interpretation; often an instant's intuition is enough to solve a century-old puzzle over which powerful minds have worn themselves out. For Luria the episode resulted in comprehending the mechanism due to which bacteria resist (or do not resist) the action of the bacteriophage: here began the genetics of bacteria, which in its turn led to the fusion of biochemistry with genetics— that is, to molecular biology.

In another context the author himself says that examples like this illustrate "how necessary it is to be flexible in scientific research," that is, ready to transfer mechanisms and concepts among distant and apparently unrelated fields. The anecdote of Newton's apple could be something more than a childish legend.

The other half of the title contains a complementary allusion. The "broken test tube" was an important test tube: it contained a bacterial culture that was the fruit of long labors, highly selected and meant for a crucial experiment. Luria at work is a hurried man: elsewhere he describes himself as frenetic, and frenetic, possessed, are many of his colleagues described in the book. He is a lover of "untilled fields"; he had no intention of wasting time reproducing the culture, and he asked a colleague for another tube with completely different bacteria. The experiment succeeds anyway, even too well, and from it springs the discovery of an unsuspected phenomenon: in short, the fact that a virus grown at the expense of a specific bacterial strain encounters resistance to its normal development, whereas it multiplies perfectly well on bacteria belonging to other species.

The phenomenon, Luria says, was the starting point for the technology of recombining DNA, that is, for modern genetic engineering, which holds great promise (and, he assures us, is devoid of dangers); and he adds, "My discovery was perfectly casual. . . . The phenomenon . . . was, so to speak, before everyone's eyes. If I had not discovered it, someone else would have discovered it. Instead my work on the fluctuation test had been something unique." Luria's justified and differentiated pride reminds us of Machiavelli's dictum that victory belongs to the strong helped by luck.

In this courageous and at times epic summary of a research and a life, one is struck by an opinion rarely found in the history of science (a history about which, strangely, Luria states that he has scarce interest, even though he liberally contributes to it with this very book). A scientist's life, the author says, is indeed conflictual, formed by battles, defeats, and victories: but the adversary is always and only the unknown, the problem to be solved, the mystery to be clarified. It is never a matter of civil war; even though of different opinions, or of different political leanings, scientists dispute each other, they compete, but they do not battle: they are bound together by a strong alliance, by the common faith "in the validity of Maxwell's or Boltzmann's equations," and by the common acceptance of Darwinism and the molecular structure of DNA.

The forger-scientist does not exist, and cannot exist, because this fraud doesn't pay: like a hardened gambler, he goes to meet his certain ruination. "Rarely do scientists vie with one another by working in hostile secrecy"; the sessions of his group at MIT "are true moments of grace," in which one communally enjoys "the human aspect of science" with the happiness of a thirsty man who stumbles onto a fountain. These are affirmations that both surprise and reassure: perhaps they're not true at every time in every place or academic environment, but they are, or have been, true for Salvador Luria, whose life they have enhanced; and therefore they can be or prove to be true again, at least for someone.

June 6, 1985

AMONG THE PEAKS
OF MANHATTAN
▪ ▪ ▪

It is easy to prove that written English is the most concise of European languages: one sees this, for example, in multilingual "directions for use" of home appliances. I don't know whether some quantitative linguist has already taken measurements on the concision of spoken languages, but after my first trip to the United States I don't think I have any doubts concerning the results: an American says twelve or fifteen things in the time it takes an Italian to say ten. Whether he makes himself understood just as well remains to be decided; in my opinion, on the average an American should admit to deafness at an earlier age than an Italian, because before him the American becomes incapable of catching certain very tenuous (only for us?) aspirations, certain evanescent vowel shadings. "Do you know English?" is a question without a precise meaning: you can read an English text with profit, possibly even of the sixteenth century, and discover yourself to be deaf and dumb before a customs agent.

▪ ▪ ▪

We too have Sunday runners, but in Central Park this is a mass phenomenon. Fat people run to slim down, slim people run to keep fit, sick people to recover, healthy people to show that they are healthy. They run wearing the earphones of their personal stereos, with their dogs (not all that enthusiastic) on the leash. A young father runs pushing ahead of him the stroller with his sleeping child; an elegant girl, the color of coffee, runs to go shopping and returns running after half an hour with plastic bags wildly dangling from her forearms. Even those who don't run wear running shoes: I've tried them; they're marvelous, light, aerated, silent, but beautiful they're not. About beauty New Yorkers, men and women, care little: they dress any which way, "casually."

Instead, they care very much about calories: that's why they run so much. But in three years all this could be changed. The press is powerful; another two or three infarctions among joggers and the fashion of the contemplative walk could explode, or even that of a sedentary life. Even on the question of calories we might be at a turn of the road; newspapers praise the Mediterranean diet, and coffee is served along with a small container full of small white and pink envelopes. In the white ones there is sugar: "only sixteen calories" is written on them, but they are still calories, and they make you fat; in the pink ones there is a disagreeable mixture of sweeteners, and a notice coldly informs that on experimental animals it has sometimes induced cancer. For the credulous there is no choice: it is either obesity or cancer; or, obviously, bitter coffee.

• • •

If I may dare set myself up as a judge of customs, and if my very kind hosts will permit me to say so, a single party is more harmful to one's health than two hundred small white or pink envelopes. At a party you stand on your feet for one or two hours with a cracker in one hand and a glass in the other, so that you don't have anything left for gesticulating or shaking the hands of those to whom you are uselessly introduced.

You are attacked from the back and sides by the garrulous and the querulous, while the serious people with whom you would like to speak are inaccessible, surrounded in their turn by the garrulous. Everyone speaks, and they speak English; in order to be understood you must raise your voice, but since everyone else does, the result is nil and acoustic fatigue increases. It is a fatigue I have never experienced before; when it prevails, expressive paralysis takes over: you are reduced to pretending that you understand and to answering with grimaces and movements of the head, and instead of speaking you are content to produce indistinct sounds; in any case the result is the same.

■ ■ ■

At both of its ends Manhattan is proud and gigantic. The more recent skyscrapers are extraordinarily beautiful; they have an insolent, lyrical, and cynical beauty. They defy the sky, and at the same time, on clear days, they reflect it from their thousand windows flush with the façade; at night, they shine like Dolomites of light. Their verticality is the fruit of speculation, but it also expresses something else: it is the work of ingenuity and audacity, and harbors within it the upward thrust that six hundred years earlier in Europe generated the Gothic cathedrals. Religion in America is a serious, energetic matter: it has little in common with asceticism. All religions here have undergone a mutation in the direction of activity and efficiency, and efficiency itself is a religion: the skyscrapers are its temples. From the roof of the double tower of the World Trade Center the view is vertiginous, as from an Alpine peak: the walls descend sheerly for four hundred meters, and down at the bottom vehicles and pedestrians swarm like frenetic insects. In the splendid bay—a tangle of islands, canals, isthmuses—the Statue of Liberty is a dwarf, but the pamphlet that describes the twin colossuses exaggerates: "You've never been so close to the stars!" Well, all you have to do is go to Lanzo* . . .

• • •

On the ground, on the sidewalks among the crystal giants, wanders a well-assorted sampling of the Human Species: no subspecies is absent, but prominent, inescapable, emerge the unaccepted, the poor devils. Men and women, whites and blacks (though blacks are in the majority), in rags or dressed with propriety, they are there sitting on the pavement or leaning against the walls; they don't ask for anything; they look into the void; smoke or chew gum in silence; some sleep among the feet of the passersby, under a roof of corrugated cardboard, others rummage through garbage cans.

They do not rummage in vain; they find half-eaten sandwiches, half-drunk Coca-Colas, shoes, clothes, books, magazines. The consumer society is prodigal; if the wind blows or it rains, they wrap themselves up in polyethylene bags that the same wind scatters about everywhere in abundance. They are, in the majority, ex-inmates of psychiatric hospitals: if they aren't dangerous, they are released and left to fend for themselves.

• • •

At the opposite extreme, at the summit of Western civilization, stand the sources of culture: museums, libraries,

---

* A hill town with a ruined castle at its peak, twenty miles west of Turin. —TRANS.

schools, and theaters. The supply of culture is "terrific"*: that's what you say, the term is positive. It is terrific in the way of quality and quantity, and it arouses reverence. My American friend gives me a diminutive explanation of this, which does not satisfy me: for the rich, founding a cultural institute is an advantage, they can deduct the amount from their tax statement.

I don't believe it is only this. There is a thirst for culture and respect for culture; in the long term, culture is perceived as a good investment. They deserve praise, those uncultivated Texas and California billionaires who invest their dollars in culture; but right now, in the short run, the fruits seem meager. American culture has very high points, it produces excellent specialists, but on the average it is lower than the European. Just like the humus on the forest floor, culture requires centuries: rapid, *instant** surrogates do not exist.

June 23, 1985

---

* English in original. —TRANS.

THE WINE OF
THE BORGIAS
▪ ▪ ▪

Among the many desires of the reader of the daily newspapers there is one whose satisfaction seems to me quite
inexpensive. It would be appropriate for the reporter
charged with the description of accidents, or, with even
greater reason, of catastrophes, to use as adequate and precise language as do his colleagues the theater critic, the
sportswriter, the financial reporter, etc. I have in mind, I'm
sure you've already guessed, two recent cases: the disaster
of Val di Fiemme and the scandal of the Austrian wines.

It would be foolish to expect that the pertinent reports
should have been immediately entrusted respectively to a
geologist and an enologist. It would be utopian to demand
a reporter who would be able to dash over to Val di Fiemme
and at the first blow unmask the lies told on the spot, in
good or bad faith, resisting the pressure of local interests,
which (as always in such cases) are enormous. And yet it
would not have been difficult even for a regular reporter to
interrogate the local people, to know and describe how the
two decantation basins were made, how large they were,
how long they had been there, and what the retaining walls

were like. In the following days we say a photograph of the installation as it had looked before the disaster: it was barely visible, but it was frightful; so that's how the two retaining walls facing the valley were, very steep, almost a sheer drop? And, as has been said, made of beaten earth? A local surveyor, a student, should not have found it difficult to make a sketch of it for us.

This isn't a request dictated only by curiosity: the citizen mustn't and doesn't intend to be satisfied with the interviews and reports of the experts; he wants to and must judge for himself, and must have the elements to do so. If there is guilt, he has the right to be indignant, but he wants to be put in a position to choose autonomously the quality, the quantity, and (above all) the target of his indignation. He distrusts or should distrust the barbaric institution of the scapegoat. He knows that the sentence will come, if it will come, at a distance of months or years, and that it will be written in the abstruse language of magistrates, which has been hybridized with the equally abtruse language of the technicians: therefore, he wants to have the possibility to form his personal opinion, even if this will not have juridical consequences.

He wants to understand, and that is his right; and he also wants to say his piece: this is a meager satisfaction that must not be taken away from him. He will in any case say his piece, but if he has been informed in a clear and correct manner, his opinion will acquire the weight that is conferred upon it by a minimum of competency.

The newspaper must make an effort to supply him with it as soon as possible: it will thus prevent hasty absolutions or condemnations; indifference, fatalism, or mob rule; dangerous smugness or unjustified fear. It is right that those responsible, if any, should be punished; but so that similar events should not be repeated, it is necessary for there to exist a widespread competence, which probably did not exist among the hundreds of people who, at all levels, had a hand in making those retaining walls; and besides, there are things that one can see better from below than from above.

The matter of the Austrian wine, at least for the moment, seems more a crooked deal than a tragedy. There is talk of only one death, and its connection to the wine that was drunk is very dubious. It is clear that in this case the Italian reporter could do nothing but repeat as best he could the information reported by his foreign colleague: but this colleague was hasty and imprecise, with a greater proclivity for stirring up a scandal than for supplying concrete data.

The claim that diethylenic glycol (not "diethylene glycol," which chemically makes no sense) is used as an antifreezing agent for the water that circulates in car radiators is incorrect: for this purpose one normally uses ethylenic glycol, which costs less and at an equal concentration yields more; it is also more toxic, but it does not appear that any of it was found in the wines.

In any case, the fact that one or the other product is used as an antifreezing agent is of no juridical relevance: stressing this, as has been done in all the newspapers of Europe, only confuses the issue. The reader asks himself, rightly, what might have induced those people to use this substance for such an unusual purpose: the same as tying salami with wire or sweeping the streets with a hoe. If the adulterator had been only one, we might think of madness, but they were many . . .

What, on the other hand, does have juridical relevance is the toxicity of diethylenic glycol. It is not very high, and for that matter it is obvious that no industrialist in his right mind would put a powerful poison in his wine. Yet, according to the toxicology textbooks, it is approximately five times more toxic than ethyl alcohol, and that's quite a lot.

In 1937 its incautious use in a medicine in America caused the death of sixty people who had ingested approximately ten grams a day over several consecutive days.

As we can see, we are at the margin of danger if it is true that some of the Austrian bottles contained sixteen grams per liter and even more. Besides, it is always difficult to foresee what effect two poisons (here, alcohol and glycol) ingested simultaneously will have; they may strengthen each other, or, conversely, one may inhibit the other; all questions with which the producer apparently didn't concern himself.

It is easily explained why diglycol was used. In many countries it is forbidden to sweeten wines with sugar or glucose; now, diglycol has a sweetish flavor that I find decidedly disagreeable, but which apparently simulates that of a number of expensive wines. From the point of view of a winemaker disposed to defraud, it has a substantial advantage: it is a modest, not at all gaudy substance whose presence does not immediately catch the eye of the analyzing chemist or the consumer.

Now, the chemist is required to check whether a product conforms to specific standards; one cannot ask him to ascertain that the product does *not* contain unpredictable extraneous substances, because there are millions of known chemical compounds. As it appears, an Austrian enologist of facile astuteness and scant professional integrity gave his many clients this fraudulent advice: "Do you want to sweeten your wines that are too dry? The law does not allow you to use sugars, which in any case would not escape analysis; so you should add diglycol, which is a little less innocuous and sweetens a little less, but no chemist will think of looking for it."

And indeed, for who knows how many years, no chemist found it: the chemist finds the compound he is looking for (when it's there—at times, if he's not very experienced, when it's not there), but to find what he's not looking for, he must be extremely skillful or shamelessly lucky.

It is less easy to explain why in certain wines there was found a percentage so low as to have no effect at all, neither positive (sweetening) nor negative (harming the drinker). But wine does go through many hands: the possibility is not to be excluded that an illegally sweetened wine was blended with genuine wine by some producer, who perhaps was unaware of the fraud: but he will not, because of this, be less responsible, and it will not now be easy for him to prove his innocence.

August 9, 1985

R E P R O D U C I N G

M I R A C L E S

■ ■ ■

It happened by chance that I read two books in a row (not
very recent ones: it is best to let books season a bit) that
dealt more or less with the same subject and took opposite
positions. One is *Viaggio nel mondo del paranormale* (Journey
Through the Paranormal World) by Piero Angela, the schol-
arly gentleman whom all TV watchers know; the other is
The Roots of Coincidence by Arthur Koestler, the author who
died a few years ago and whose novels have formed a generation of Europeans.

The first makes a clean sweep: paranormal phenomena
do not exist. Telepathy, precognition, spiritualism, astrol-
ogy, psychokinesis, etc., are all products of skillful trickery
or self-delusion. Their frequent validation by illustrious
physicists during the last hundred years proves nothing:
physicists are accustomed to the "good faith" of the facts
they observe, they themselves are in good faith, subtle in
interpreting experimental data, naïve before the subtlety of
charlatans. Uri Geller, the spoon bender, is a very skillful
charlatan; Kirlian, the Russian who photographs the "aura"

that surrounds leaves, seeds, insects, and human hands, is an exalted ignoramus.

In the long list there is not a phenomenon that a good magician cannot reproduce: if he is honest, he declares himself to be what he is, a professional trickster; if he is dishonest, he claims that he possesses superhuman gifts. The best exegetes are not the scientists but in fact the magicians, especially those who have reached the end of their careers; but they too (and on this point Angela's book is somewhat lacking in good taste), out of professional solidarity with their younger colleagues, refuse to reveal the key to their most astonishing routines.

After the books that made him famous throughout the world, Koestler took a road that surprised many: he began a war against the established positions of official science. He never was a physicist or a biologist, but he had always possessed an enviable polemical verve; thanks to his fame, he had access to sources (also personnel) unavailable to most, and he built for himself quite a respectable culture. In the book I have mentioned, his thesis is deliberately scandalous: paranormal phenomena exist, we live among them, but being one-eyed and, what is more, confused by established science, we do not notice this.

The Galileo case is recurrent: one does not want to look through the telescope, anyone who looks does not want to see and thus does not see, the neo-Aristotelians do their best to gag or excommunicate the seers. And yet modern physics is so strange that its strangeness should render us less incredulous: if we believe in the uncertainty principle, in the wave/corpuscle double aspect of particles, in the curvature of space, and in the relativity of time, we cannot reject the equally strange data that rain down on us from the world of the paranormal. If physicists are credulous, more power to them: skepticism is more a hindrance than a filter.

In the competition I would declare Angela the winner, but on points. He is right when he helps us unclutter our horizon of the foolishnesses and deceptions, but it is imprudent to be so drastic: an often-quoted statement of Prince Hamlet comes to mind, and a more recent one by Arthur Clarke according to which if a scientist of great fame declares an undertaking possible, one must believe him, but if he declares an undertaking impossible, it is wiser to distrust him. For example: Angela denies that water-diviners have any power whatsoever; yet an authoritative Swiss newspaper a few years ago published the news that Roche (yes, the well-known pharmaceutical company) pays a regular salary to two diviners and sends them all over the world to search for water for its new plants. The Swiss are people with their feet well planted on the ground, and they do not like to throw away francs: before hiring the diviners, they put them through a serious examination and observed that under specific conditions, which can be easily reproduced, the diviners do find water without making mistakes.

The point is precisely this, the possibility of reproduction. Koestler uses an expedient known to orators for centuries: he accumulates avalanches of facts, some well documented, others not so well, and still others known only by hearsay; in short, he counts on the mass effect, but his "coincidences" are never capable of being reproduced. A *single* clairvoyant with consistent abilities would be enough to break the lottery, Monte Carlo, and all the bookies in the world. Koestler's argument on the strangeness of physics can impress only the naïve: the phenomena observed or unleashed by the physicists of today are strange certainly, but they can be reproduced; in Europe, America, or China, a physicist who describes an experiment that cannot be reproduced is simply laughed at.

And yet . . . and yet phenomena that cannot be reproduced do exist: each of us has experienced them. The physicist correctly neglects them, because just as science is not made on the individual fact, neither is it made on sporadic, erratic facts: but it does not forget them. It tries to purify them of all emotional ingredients and to free itself from false memories and hallucinations; it avoids wasting time in explaining phenomena whose existence is dubious, but it builds for itself, year after year, its own mental and private museum in which, for future memory, are a number of indubitable facts that science does not know how to explain. I have never been a physicist, but I have not forgotten thirty years of militancy in minor chemistry, and my private museum is not mental but material. It contains three objects that I will describe and that wait (up to now in vain) for someone to explain their origin.

The first is fifteen years old, and it is not picturesque: it is a lump of semifused synthetic resin, hard as wood. It comes from a dessicator in which air was introduced at 65° centigrade: the operation had been performed a thousand times without any damage, at that temperature the resin was regularly dessicated. Only twice in twenty years did it happen that just in one corner of the dessicator the resin heated up spontaneously to the point of fusion; once it actually became incandescent.

The second is eighteen years old, and it is a section of enameled copper wire; the enamel, of a most common type, is blackish and does not adhere to metal. Up to this point, there's nothing unusual, because the sample comes from a continuous oven in the extinguishing phase, in which the progress of the wire is halted and is left to burn quietly on the spot. What is strange is that only twice in my career as a wire enamelist, the enamel detached itself not in flakes but rather in the shape of a propeller with at least a hundred volutes and a thread as regular as if made by the threading machine.

The third object is very pretty. It is (alas!) almost forty years old, and it is, or rather was, a small steel sphere approximately twelve millimeters in diameter. It was part of the load in a ball mill, that is, a large drum into which are loaded all at once the components of an enamel and special "balls" of cast iron, ceramic, or steel; the mill turns slowly, and the friction among the balls disperses the pigment in the varnish. This was just after the war, and for lack of better that load was composed of ball bearings that perhaps had been discarded after testing. As usual, when the mill began to grind less effectively the balls were extracted to be replaced by new ones; well, in good part, they were no longer spherical but presented twelve regular pentagon facets; in short, they were pentagonododecahedrons with rounded corners. I asked many colleagues, and as far as I can tell this incident never occurred in other mills or in other plants. Why did it happen, and why only that once?

If the three *corpora delicti*, improbable but certainly not paranormal, were not there to prove by their obstinate presence that they exist, I would think my memory of the three events that gave birth to them had become contaminated or magnified with the passing of the years, as happens with the memory of premonitory dreams.

September 15, 1985

T H E   M A N   W H O   F L I E S
■ ■ ■

This is in regard to the competition announced by *Tutto-scienze*, a competition in experiments that are viable in the absence of gravity: unfortunately, I am too old to participate, but the experiment I would most like to attempt would be that of finding myself, if only for moments, released from the weight of my body. It's not that this weight is excessive (it fluctuates within a more than reasonable range), yet I am intensely envious of the weightless astronauts whom we are permitted to see on our television screens for a few, very precious moments. They seem at their ease, like fish in water: they move about elegantly in their cabin, which by now is quite spacious, pushing themselves off with small taps of their hands against invisible supports, and navigate smoothly through the air, landing safely at their work stations.

At other times we've seen them converse naturally among themselves, one of them "head up," the other "head down" (but, clearly, in orbit there no longer is an up or down); or we see them playing childish pranks on each other: one with his thumbnail shot off a piece of candy that flew slowly, slowly in a straight line and neatly entered his colleague's open mouth. Other times we've seen an astronaut squeeze water into the air from a plastic container: the water neither fell nor dispersed but settled in a roundish mass, which then, obeying its albeit weak surface tension, lazily assumed the shape of a sphere. What did they do with it afterward? It can't have been easy to get rid of it without damaging the delicate devices crowding the walls.

I asked myself what we are waiting for to produce a documentary by sewing together these visions, admirably transmitted by the satellites in flashing flight above our heads and our atmosphere. A film made like this, drawn from American and Soviet sources and with an intelligent commentary, would teach many things to everyone. It would certainly be more successful than the many insipidities that are administered to us, and even more successful than the blue films.

I've often asked myself also what meaning they have, and how they have been carried out, the various experiments and simulation courses to which all aspiring astronauts are subjected, and about which the journalists talk as if there were nothing to them. Apparently, the only thinkable technique would be to lock the candidates in a free-falling vehicle: an airplane or an elevator such as the one Einstein had postulated for the thought experiment to illustrate restricted relativity.

But an airplane, even when falling vertically, is slowed down by the resistance of the air, and an elevator (more appropriately, a descender) is slowed down also, by the friction against the roller guide shoes. In both cases the absence of weight would not be complete; even in the more favorable case, the quite terrifying case of an airplane that plunges straight down from a height of ten or twenty kilometers, possibly with the help of its engines over the terminal stretch, and which, when all is said and done, would not last longer than a few dozen seconds, too little for training and for the recording of physiological data. And besides, there would have to be some way of applying the brakes . . .

And yet, almost all of us have experienced a "simulation" of this decidedly nonterrestrial condition. We've experienced it in a youthful dream: in its most typical version, the dreamer realizes with happy astonishment that flying is as easy as walking or swimming. How could he be so stupid as not to have thought of it before? All you have to do is row with the palms of your hands, and there! you take off from the floor, advance without effort, turn about, avoid obstacles, slip through windows and doors with precision, glide out into the open: not with the frenetic beating of sparrows' wings, not with the voracious and strident haste of swallows, but with the silent majesty of eagles and clouds. From where does this anticipation of today's concrete reality come to us? Perhaps it is a memory of the species, inherited from our aquatic reptile forebears. Or perhaps this dream is instead a forecast of an unspecified future in which the umbilical tearing away from the pull of Mother Earth will be gratuitous and obvious, and there will prevail a manner of locomotion much nobler than that on our two complicated, discontinuous legs, filled with internal frictions and at the same time in need of the external friction of the feet against the ground.

Of this so persistently dreamed-of weightlessness I remember an illustrious poetic version, Geryon's episode in Canto 17 of the *Inferno*. The "proud animal" reconstructed by Dante on classical models, but also on the basis of the hints of medieval bestiaries, is imaginary and at the same time splendidly real. It escapes weight. While waiting for his two strange passengers, only one of whom is subject to gravity, it leans against the shore with its front quarters, but its lethal tail floats free "in the void" like the stern of a Zeppelin anchored to its mooring. Dante, at the beginning, declares that he is afraid of it, but then the magical descent over Malebolge captures the entire attention of the poet-scientist, who is paradoxically intent on a naturalistic study of his fictitous creature and describes with precision its monstrous and symbolic epidermis.

The brief reportage is singularly accurate, down to the detail confirmed by the pilots of modern hang-gliders: since this is a silent gliding flight, the traveler's perception of speed comes not from the rhythm of the wings or the noise but only from the sensation of the air that "blows into his face and from below." Perhaps also Dante, unconsciously, has reproduced here the universal dream of weightless flight, to which the psychoanalyst attributes problematic and immodest meanings.

The ease with which man adjusts to the absence of weight is a fascinating mystery. If one thinks that, for many, traveling by sea, or even only by car, is the cause of vexing discomfort, one can only be perplexed. During months of living in space, the astronauts complained only of passing discomforts, and the physicians who examined them after the exploit found only a slight decalcification of the bones and a transitory atrophy of muscles and heart: in short, the same effect as a period in bed; and yet nothing in our long evolutionary history could have prepared us for such an unnatural condition as nongravity.

So we do have vast and unforeseen margins of safety: the visionary project (one of his many) presented by Freeman Dyson in his book *Disturbing the Universe*, of a humanity migrating among the stars on ships with gigantic sails propelled free of charge by the light of the stars, may have its limits but not that of weightlessness: our poor body, so defenseless when confronted by swords, guns, and viruses, is spaceproof.

December 24, 1985

A B O U T   G O S S I P
■ ■ ■

I've read with interest that the New York publisher Alfred
A. Knopf has published a book by Patricia Mayer Spacks
entitled *Gossip*. I immediately ordered it and am impatiently
awaiting its arrival, but at the same time I feel vaguely frus-
trated because for a long time I've been flirting with the
idea of writing something on this subject. It would appear,
however, that the book is no less than a historical and so-
ciological treatise, while I would be satisfied with creating
a kind of taxonomy of gossip, that is, a classification, as has
always been done with plants and animals.

In the hope of not committing an involuntary plagia-
rism, since in fact I have not yet read that book, I set forth
here the index of the book that I haven't written and that
I will probably never write. It should be said in passing:
to write the general or analytical indexes or the fore- or
afterwords, or better yet, putative reviews of the books one
has in mind, would be an educational exercise, besides being
supremely economical for the reader, indeed for the non-
reader. This exercise has been practiced at length with hon-
esty and success by Rodolfo Wilcock.

In the introduction, I would not be satisfied with the definition to be found in the standard Italian dictionary, the Zingarelli—"indiscreet and malicious talk about someone." It seems to me essential to point out that the malice must stop at a low level: in its common acceptance, attributing a murder or a rape to someone is not gossip. In short, there exists a quite well defined border between gossip and malicious talk, and between this and slander (or accusation, if the crime exists). Furthermore, in the concept of gossip there seems to me to be implied an element of secrecy: you gossip in privacy with one other person, or at the most in a circle with a few persons; in short, among intimates. It wouldn't even seem appropriate to me to call gossip anything spread by print or TV. In sum, gossip is a liquor that must be poured in small doses into one ear, or possibly into more than one, but not into too many—otherwise, its name changes. Having said this, I would announce the following chapters:

1. *Why people gossip.* I know something that you do not know; by transmitting it to you, I'm comforted because I have the pleasant impression of going up by one rung. I've become a teacher, a professor, even though for just a few minutes and on a small subject. Naturally, you the recipient are fully entitled (and feel compelled) to transform yourself, in turn, into a professor, retransmitting my message, or any other one, and consoling yourself with this small pleasure for your unpleasant experiences.

2. *Plain gossip.* This consists simply in relaying the message to the recipient without imposing restraints or limitations. It is the most widespread type. Since the recipients are more than one, this gossip spreads in a ramified pattern and thus, tendentially, follows the exponential law. It has, that is, the tendency to invade the ecumenical area, as happened with

the chains of Saint Anthony; generally it does not achieve much, first of all because it enters into competition with other, more recent and therefore more appetizing messages and so tends to fade away; second, because every time it is passed along, the transmitted information is degraded, becoming vague and at the same time richer in spurious or suspect detail. The information turns into hearsay, hearsay to the point of becoming ennobled as legend. It is rare for gossip, like slander, to change from a "slight breeze" into a "cannon blast."

3. *Restricted gossip.* "I'm telling only you: don't tell anyone else." In the eleventh chapter of Manzoni's novel *The Betrothed*, with regard to the botched plan that would have Lucia seeking shelter in the monastery at Monza, the author observes about this scheme: "Anyone who were to take [it] in the strict sense of the words would immediately cut off the flow of consolation. But general practice demands that only the trusted friend be obliged not to confide the secret to anyone who is not an equally trusted friend, imposing the same condition on him. So, from trusted friend to trusted friend, the secret travels along that immense chain until it reaches the ear of the one or the many whom the first person who spoke never intended it to reach."

4. *The exclusion of the* de quo, *which aims precisely at avoiding the above result.* "Tell whoever you like, but don't tell X"—where X, generally speaking, is the object of the gossip, or is somehow implicated. This variant is dealt with in the popular saying "The last to know is the (betrayed) husband." It has been experimentally observed that in general that is exactly how things go: perhaps because the gossiper feels spiritually akin to the faithless spouse (he too, in fact, is doing something illicit: but sympathy for the unfaithful is common to all civilizations and literatures, in the teeth

of both the laws and morality) or because if he were to reveal the fact to whom it is naturally directed, he would put too quick an end to the game; or because, on the other hand, he fears the consequences of the revelation, as when Macbeth brutally attacks the messenger who brings him the news about Birnam Wood coming to the castle of Dunsinane. If matters proceed normally, that is, the target of the gossip does not hear it, the graph of this type of gossip assumes a characteristic form: a thick tangle of fine lines that surround a small white area without penetrating.

5. *The denied source.* "Go ahead and tell, but don't say you got it from me," or a variant, "Don't tell who told you." This denotes extreme pusillanimity on the part of the gossiper; if it appears, even only once, along the gossip's chain, it interrupts it irremediably, frustrating any and all attempts at reconstruction or denial, or even retaliation by the victim.

I would dedicate the conclusion to the relationship between the credibility of the message and its diffusion. These two entities are not proportional, nor do they grow together: indeed, we can see the vitality of absurd information. This is part of the extraodinary intrinsic vitality of the phenomenon. Gossip prospers in the soil of idleness, forced or voluntary: in prisons, jails, hospices, barracks, "village Saturdays"; and by the same token in resorts, on cruises, in drawing rooms. It is irrepressible, it is a force of human nature. Anyone who has obeyed nature by transmitting a piece of gossip experiences the explosive relief that accompanies the satisfying of a primary need.

June 24, 1986

J A C K   L O N D O N ' S
B U C K
▪ ▪ ▪

Einaudi's prestigious "Writers Translated by Writers" series reached its nineteenth volume with an unexpected gift: a new edition of *The Call of the Wild* by Jack London in the beautiful, rigorous translation by Gianni Celati. The book is very well known, and precisely because of this it has many surprises in store for the reader, or rather, for the rereader, no matter what generation he belongs to. A book one knows is read in a different way from a new book: one already knows "how it ends," and so one is more critical of its events and more attentive to the details.

Its authenticity immediately leaps to the eye. The *très curieux* London—a writer long considered marginal, popular, in short, a stray dog within the illustrious American literary tradition—has drawn from his brief adventure as a prospector for gold in Alaska a fabulous wealth of storytelling experiences, and he is a great storyteller. Nothing of what he relates smacks of the trite, of something written at the desk by borrowing from books or by thinking things out. The savage world in which he found himself immersed is decanted into his best books with the powerful immediacy of

Primo Levi

lived experience: here we have no Verne, no Salgari, but rather a man who has fought the struggle for life and for survival to the bitter end and has taken from this struggle a reason for writing.

With unerring intuition he poured this experience of his into a dog, and I believe that this dog has no rivals in world literature, precisely because he is not a literary dog. Buck, a well-to-do dog, master at home on a splendid California estate, is at once canine and human, as are all dogs whom fate and their owners have treated neither too badly nor too well. He emanates dignity and respectability: more than a subject of Judge Miller, he is his peer, companion; he has an instinctive knowledge of his rights and his duties. But at the turn of the century, at the time of the gold fever, all robust dogs are threatened: they have an incredible commercial value, they can be stolen, traded, and carried off up there, where it is no longer civil law that counts but, rather, the law of the cudgel and of the fang. They must become sled dogs or perish.

Thanks to his physical and moral vigor, Buck passes the first test, that of the deportation, an interminable journey by train and then by boat, and he arrives in a hostile new country: no longer the sun of California but snow on the ground and in the air. He is tamed: he learns that a man armed with a cudgel is invincible. His dignity is not extinguished but is transformed: he learns that he must adjust, learn new and terrible things, that he must distrust everyone, but especially his companions, who are already experienced sled dogs—if he is not as fast as they are, his daily ration will be instantly stolen from him; that at night the fire and the tent are not for him: he must learn, and he does learn, to dig himself a hole in the snow, where his animal warmth will allow him to endure the freezing arctic.

He must learn his job, and here London strikes masterful tones. Each of these dogs is of a hundred different breeds, and each, yoked every day to the sled, has a surprisingly credible personality of his own. An ethologist ahead of his time, London has penetrated canine psychology with a completely modern profundity. Rivals among themselves and yet gregarious, the sled dogs "elect" a chief, the leader of the pack, the dog at the head of the team. He must be the strongest but also the most experienced: the job of pulling the sled is a job that must be accepted, and Spitz, the head dog, enforces and speeds up this acceptance. He punishes anyone who hinders the work, bites the stragglers, breaks up the fights with his undisputed authority.

Buck understands, he learns, but he does not accept Spitz's authority: he feels within himself not only the perpetual hunger for food but also the hunger for primacy. But he does accept pulling the sled: "And though the work was hard he found he did not particularly despise it. He was surprised at the eagerness which animated the whole team, and which was communicated to him." This is work as the last refuge and as the alternative to servitude. How can one not remember Solzhenitsyn's story *One Day in the Life of Ivan Denisovich* and that wall that prisoners gladly build, struggling against the freezing cold of another arctic? Dave and Sol-leks, old sled dogs, are passive and indifferent, but when they are harnessed to the sled they become "alert and active, anxious that the work should go well, and fiercely irritable with whatever, by delay or confusion, retarded that work. The toil of the traces seemed the supreme expression of their being, and all that they lived for and the only thing in which they took delight." Work is a form of intoxication: they feel heartbroken when they are excluded from it. Here in germ is the intuition of the human pathology of early retirement.

Buck is different, he feels being reborn within him "the

dominant primordial beast," he subtly provokes the leader of the pack, encourages disorder, until he openly challenges Spitz. This is the master page of the short book, and it is the fiercest: during a freezing night, surrounded by the starved but neutral pack, Spitz and Buck confront each other and Buck gets the better of him, thanks to his cleverness as a fighter: the loser is devoured on the spot by his former underlings. The next morning, Buck forces acceptance on his human masters: he has killed the leader of the team, he is the new team leader. He will be a chief (a *Kapo?*) even more efficient than Spitz, better at keeping order and discovering dangers along the track.

■ ■ ■

Then the team changes owners, and in spring, when the ice is most treacherous, they end up in the hands of three inexperienced men. Hunger, weariness, whippings: Buck's dignity rebels, the dog mutinies, he "knows" whom he must and whom he mustn't obey. Subjected to a deadly beating, he is saved by Thornton, the good prospector, and grows attached to him with total, exclusive love, the love of which only dogs are capable: and it's precisely here that, in my opinion, the book becomes weak. This devotion is excessive: where did the "dominant beast" go?

Nor are other pages convincing into which are filtered ill-digested Darwinian reminiscences. Thornton dies, pierced by Indian arrows, and Buck, his last link with the civilization of men broken, harkens to the call of the wild, that is, the howl of the wolves: within him, as an evolutionary force, he senses the wolf's blood. Despite his so very different life story, he runs with the pack until he become part of it, indeed becomes its leader. California, the sled, Thornton—all are forgotten, and Buck's story, as Celati remarks, becomes (though only, I believe, after this turn of the plot) myth. Buck's blood has prevailed over the blood of the wolves, to the point of modifying their appearance: a new generation of wolves with canine hair is born. Buck has become the Phantom Dog, ferocious, nocturnal savager of prey and men: but every summer he goes in pilgrimage to the spot where Thornton is buried, the only creature whom the dog-turned-wolf ever loved. Come now: this is a bit too human.

January 11, 1987

ADAM'S CLAY

▪ ▪ ▪

How difficult it is to understand a book that is admittedly misunderstood by its own author! This thought has accompanied me all through the arduous (but fruitful) reading of a recently published book, *Seven Clues to the Origin of Life: A Scientific Detective Story*, by A. Graham Cairns-Smith. Despite the loftiness of its aim, this book is a popularization of an important, bold idea.

As one can see, the title itself is at once an understatement and full of promises. The origin of life on Earth is not just any problem, it is *the* problem over which all scientists, not only biologists, have racked their brains ever since the existence of science. There is no lack of proposed solutions; before Spallanzani and Pasteur, the answer of the classics and of Aristotle was considered correct, that life is born by spontaneous generation from corrupt matter, frogs from mud, flies from dirt. Only the nineteenth century was to make a clean sweep of such a naïve affirmation: compared to microorganisms, frogs and worms are organisms too complex to form themselves "by themselves." But what about the microorganisms, then?

The electron microscope, together with the discoveries of genetics, was to give a stern and disappointing answer: even microorganisms are extremely complex, they are "high-technology" machines; it would be just as absurd to think that they are born by spontaneous generation as that a watch can be built by shaking together its minutest components. The fundamental and unitary components of life, the nucleotides of nucleic acid present in molds as well as beech trees, giraffes, and ourselves, cannot be formed on their own; it is enough to think of the number and delicacy of the steps that the chemist must perform to build a single one, and of the precautions he must take to avoid its self-destruction.

And yet, if one does not want to resort to supernatural hypotheses, there certainly must have been one spontaneous generation. Toward the middle of this century a curious experiment by Miller had aroused great hopes. By subjecting a blend of methane, water, ammonia, and hydrogen to "artificial storms" (high temperatures, charges of electricity), it was possible to obtain the bricks of organic life: traces of amino acids and nucleotides. Everyone was exultant, both chemists and laymen. So a road was open: the creative act postulated by all religions and metaphysics was not necessary, life could have been born by itself, from the primordial soup constituted by the ocean of the newborn Earth.

A more cautious examination was to demolish these hopes. Bricks are not enough to build a house: you need a plan, a direction, a design. The key to life is ordered complexity, and the complex is not born from the simple. Nor did it make much sense to postulate that order came from the cosmos, as Fred Hoyle recently maintained: who, then, might have introduced it into the cosmos? Either the problem is shifted from one place to another or you must have recourse to God. Now, scientists have respect for God and for those who believe in Him, but they are reluctant to admit a premature intervention before having exhausted all other possible explanations.

Graham formulates a fascinating new hypothesis. He sets out from an allegory. Let us imagine that in an uninhabited area we find an arch of stones that support each other. The first hypothesis is that this is a human work, or at any rate that of a superior intelligence: an arch does not build itself by itself. Yet it is possible to think of a different, "natural" mechanism. To build an arch, it is convenient also for man to arrange the stones on a substratum, a scaffolding of wood or stone that is later destroyed. It is improbable, but not impossible, that also the arch we have found rested on a spontaneous scaffolding of stones, which a flood later carried away. And what if the same had happened in the creation of life? If, that is, the primal life were what remains of a construction in which mingled basic elements later on disappeared?

Graham believes that he has found this substratum, and that he has discovered it in a material that is very abundant in life, complex in structure but extremely varied in its forms (as, in fact, the electron microscope reveals), and besides all this ennobled by an illustrious Biblical mention: primeval life, protolife, supposedly was based not on carbon but rather on silicates of clay: yes, the same clay used by God the Father to fashion the first man.

The many clays studied by Graham reveal surprising capacities: they assimilate material from ambient water, they grow, they subdivide, they repair damage; furthermore, they know how to dispose themselves in slats of an evanescent thinness, in small tubes, in porous heaps: they are the equivalent of minuscule chemistry laboratories with their equipment for filtration, distillation, concentration, etc.; above all, they can multiply by reproducing themselves; and how many of these laboratories may be at work simultaneously! Nor does Graham shy away from the typically vital capacity to extract carbon and nitrogen from the atmosphere in order to "make them organic"; when illuminated by the sun, iron salts transform carbon dioxide into formic acid, and titanium oxide transforms nitrogen into ammonia: the rest is easy . . .

Not easy, indeed frightfully difficult, is the next step: how to go from self-duplicating clays to organic life such as has triumphed today. I must admit (but Graham also admits) that here things become quite confused. The step was supposedly gradual; a form of "usurpation," as if from a hemp rope one were to take out, one by one, the original fibers in order to replace them with nylon fibers. There supposedly was a long period of coexistence of the embryonic life of clays and organic life, with the latter finally prevailing. Like nucleic acids and proteins, clay particles are in fact able to fold upon themselves, assuming configurations that are characteristic and specific and, what is more, transmissible to other particles they come into contact with.

Are you, the reader who tries to read the great book of nature backwards, satisfied? I am, despite everything, despite the fact that the author himself manifests his doubts with dozens of ifs, buts, and perhapses on every page. From this difficult and convulsed reading I have issued with a vague impression, that of having witnessed a breakthrough, perhaps comparable to those of Newton and Darwin. Or perhaps instead this is only a "working hypothesis," a scaffolding precisely, that will in any case be demolished whether the arch stands or collapses. In any event, a new idea has been launched, halfway between chemistry and geology, and we know today how fruitful hybridizations between different disciplines are.

February 15, 1987

THE SPIDER'S SECRET
■ ■ ■

It seems strange to many people, and it is beginning to seem strange to me as well: for thirty years, that is, for the entire active center of my life, I've worked at producing varnishes—liquid substances that, when spread in a thin layer, after a certain period of time, become solid, either spontaneously or when heated. It seems to me just as strange that varnishes are displacing Auschwitz in the "ground floor" of my memory: I realize this from my dreams, from which the *Lager* has by now disappeared and in which, with increasing frequency, I am faced with a varnish maker's problem that I cannot solve.

It is understood that the definition of varnish that I have just given is a bit summary. When beer and seawater evaporate into the air in a thin layer, they too leave behind a solid residue, yet they cannot be called varnishes. In short, a varnish must have various other general and special qualities that everyone knows, so it is useless to go to the trouble of defining it here.

In the course of my career I have had many curious problems: for example, developing for application to the insulators of high-tension electroducts a varnish that would change color distinctly and irreversibly, so that one could see from the ground that the insulation had overheated, however briefly. Many years earlier a more frivolous problem had been presented to me. A dandyish young man who passed himself off as a producer of cosmetics had asked me to work up for him a colored "evening" varnish to be applied to the teeth in the same way you apply polish to the nails. After the evening was over, it would have to be removed with a nontoxic solvent: in fact, with ethyl alcohol. I was supposed to develop the product, and then he would launch a high-powered advertising campaign. I don't think I devoted more than a quarter hour's study to this request; on my own teeth I tested a green enamel more or less suited to the purpose, and the effect seemed so disgusting to me that I immediately telephoned the dandy and told him I was not available for his project. Another time I was asked for a black, glossy, fast-drying, and very low priced varnish. It did not have to be weather-resistant, my client insisted—he was a coffin manufacturer.

Aside from these eccentricities, the phenomena in which a liquid becomes solid still have a particular hold on me: you cannot ask a soldier to forget his battlefields. A varnish factory is also a factory of stalactites, and this too is a passage from liquid to solid. But natural stalactites form with the passing of millennia, whereas for ours weeks are enough. Often the shutters do not close tight; the drops of varnish that come out of the vats have time to solidify before falling, and from this are born graceful drippings with a hornlike consistency, which are ruthlessly broken off and thrown into the garbage. They can be chunky or slim, transparent or colored; at times they are forked or in bunches. They grow slowly and silently, like upside-down mushrooms.

The passage from liquid to solid is never a banal spectacle, as anyone knows who has watched the cooling of molten iron in an ingot mold, or the setting of red-hot lava. A "cooking" of wax that solidifies in a cauldron spontaneously assumes the shape of an elegant crater, whereas a cooking of rosin, since it preserves a certain fluidity until it solidifies, congeals into a shiny, even mirror, "the mirror of Narcissus." And what could I say about the freezing of water? Often a dirty city puddle, after a winter's night, is transformed into a delicate mesh of dentilated crystals dozens of centimeters long; and the fact that one will never find two snow crystals that are exactly the same is proverbial.

We are at the edge of a thicket of symbolic connotations, due to which solidification is from time to time experienced as positive or negative, reassuring or deadly. Blood coagulates: in the majority of cases in a beneficent manner, at other times (inside the vascular system) producing a fatal thrombosis, but it is always a dramatic phenomenon and, what's more, fabulously complicated. And everyone has heard of rigor mortis.

The most admirable solidification I ever ran into is, however, something else altogether; it is that of the thread of spiders, tiny animals full of resources about which (I have already described this) I have strongly ambivalent emotions. Not one of the schemes one normally encounters applies to the instantaneous solidifying of the spider's thread. Could it be a simple congealing, just as water, iron, and wax solidify when they are cooled below a certain temperature? Certainly not: the spider's temperature is always the same as that of the environment in which it lives, and its reservoir cannot be warmer than the air. The spider's threader, seen under the microscope, closely resembles the one through which nylon thread is drawn, but this is an illusory analogy: above the latter there is the melted nylon, at a heat of more than 250°.

Can it be evaporating a solvent, as is the case with varnishes? No: no solvent has ever been found in the spider's tiny body except water, which is slow to evaporate; while, on the other hand, the solidification of the thread is instantaneous, it changes from liquid to solid as soon as it issues from the threader; otherwise, the spider could not hang from it. Furthermore, if we had here the evaporation of a watery solution, the thread would remain soluble in water, which it does not; even when just woven, the spider's web has good resistance to rain and dew.

Could a polymerization be taking place, that is, could long and therefore solid molecules be forming, setting out from a "soup" of small molecules contained in the spider's glands? Chemists do not know of any polymerization process that takes place in a fraction of a second and, so to speak, "on command," that is, on the simple passage from a confined environment into the open air. They do know of processes in which solids are formed by blending two liquids, but the spider possesses only one kind of raw material.

The solution of the problem has been known for only a few years, and it is of disarming simplicity. The liquid secreted by the spider's glands and stored above the threaders becomes solid when it is subjected to traction. It is composed of molecules already long enough to be solid, but they are rolled up, and so they glide one on top of the other; that is, they are a liquid, even though very viscous. But the spider secretes his thread always and only under traction: he "stretches" his thread. Now, this liquid is so fine and specific that a modest lengthening of its floss is sufficient to provoke its irreversible solidification: the tangled molecules distend and become parallel threads. This is the same mechanism that all caterpillars use in building a cocoon for themselves: this is how silk is born.

No chemist has yet succeeded in reproducing so elegant, simple, and clean a process. We have surpassed and violated nature in many fields, but we still have much to learn from nature.

November 9, 1986

THE DISPUTE AMONG
GERMAN HISTORIANS
■ ■ ■

The polemic under way in Germany between those who tend to banalize the Nazi slaughter (Nolte, Hillgruber) and those who insist on its uniqueness (Habermas and many others) cannot leave us indifferent. The thesis of the former is not new: there have been slaughters in all centuries, especially at the beginning of ours, and above all against "class enemies" in the Soviet Union, therefore near German borders. During the Second World War we Germans did nothing but adapt ourselves to a horrendous but already established procedure—an "Asiatic" practice comprised of slaughter, mass deportation, ruthless exile to hostile regions, torture, and the separation of families. Our single innovation was purely technological: we invented the gas chamber.

It should be said in passing: it is precisely this innovation that has been denied by the "revisionists," the followers of Faurisson; hence, the two theses complement each other in a system of historical interpretation that cannot help but be alarming.

Now, the Soviets cannot be absolved. First the slaughter of the Kulaks and then the obscene trials and innumerable cruel acts against real or presumed enemies of the people are very grave events that led to the political isolation of the Soviet Union, which with various shadings (and with the forced parenthesis of the war) lasts to this day. But no juridical system absolves one murderer because other murderers exist in the house across the street. Moreover, there is no doubt that these were events within the Soviet Union that nobody from the outside would have been able to prevent except by means of an all-out war.

In short, the new German revisionists tend to present the Hitlerian slaughters as a preventive defense against an "Asiatic" invasion. This thesis seems to me extremely flimsy. It would be very difficult to show that the Russians intended to invade Germany; on the contrary, they feared her, as was proven by the hasty Ribbentrop-Molotov Pact; and they rightly feared her, as was demonstrated by the subsequent and sudden German attack in 1941. Furthermore, it is hard to see how the "political" slaughters carried out by Stalin could find their mirror image in the Hitlerian slaughter of the Jewish people, when it is well known that before Hitler's rise to power the German Jews were profoundly German, intimately integrated in the nation, considered enemies only by Hitler himself and the few fanatics who originally followed him. The identification of Judaism with Bolshevism, Hitler's *idée fixe*, had no objective basis whatsoever, especially in Germany, where, it is well known, the enormous majority of Jews belonged to the bourgeois class.

That "the gulag came before Auschwitz" is true; but one cannot forget that the aims of the two infernos were not the same. The first was a massacre among peers; it was not based on racial primacy and did not divide humanity into supermen and submen. The second was founded on an ideology saturated with a world split in two, "we" the masters on one side, all the rest on the other: at their service or exterminated because racially inferior. This contempt for the fundamental equality of rights among all human beings is shown by a mass of symbolic details, starting with the Auschwitz tattoo and going all the way to the use in the gas chambers of the poison originally produced to disinfest the holds of ships invaded by rats. The sacrilegious exploitation of the corpses, and their ashes, remains the unique appanage of Hitlerian Germany, and to this day, despite those who try to blur its contours, it constitutes its emblem.

It is true, of course, that in the gulag mortality was fearfully high, but it was, so to speak, a by-product, tolerated with cynical indifference: the primary purpose, barbaric though it was, had a rationality of its own, consisting in the reinvention of a slave-based economy destined for the "construction of socialism." Now, even from Solzhenitsyn's pages, quivering with well-justified fury, nothing appears that is even close to Treblinka and Chelmno, which did not supply labor and were not concentration camps but "black holes" meant for men, women, and children guilty only of being Jewish, where one got off the trains only in order to enter the gas chambers, from which no one ever came out alive. The Soviet invaders of Germany, after the martyrdom of their country (do you remember, among a hundred details, the ruthless siege of Leningrad?), were thirsting for revenge, and stained themselves with serious crimes, but among them there were no *Einsatzkommandos* ordered to machine-gun the civilian population and bury it in enormous mass graves often dug by the victims themselves; nor for that matter had they ever planned the annihilation of the German people, against whom they then harbored a justified desire for reprisal.

Nobody has ever reported that in the gulag there took place "selections" like those in the German *Lager*, described so often, during which, by one glance at the front and one at the back, the SS physicians (physicians!) decided who could still work and who should go to the gas chambers. And I don't see how this "innovation" can be considered marginal and attenuated by an "only." It was not an "imitation" of "Asiatic" methods, it was perfectly European, the gas was produced by illustrious German chemical plants; and to other German plants went the hair of the massacred women; and to German banks went the gold of the teeth extracted from the corpses. All of this is specifically German, and no German ought to forget it; nor ought he forget that in Nazi Germany, and only there, even children and the moribund were led to an atrocious death, in the name of an abstract and ferocious radicalism that has no equal in modern times.

In the ambiguous polemic now in progress it is of no relevance that the Allies share a great portion of responsibility. It is true that no democratic nation offered asylum to the endangered or expelled Jews. It is true that the Americans refused to bomb the railroad tracks that led to Auschwitz (while they abundantly bombed the contiguous industrial area); it is also true that the lack of assistance by the Allies was due to sordid motivations, that is, the fear of having to shelter and feed millions of refugees or survivors. But one cannot speak of a true complicity, and the moral and juridical difference between those who do and those who allow it to be done remains immeasurable.

If today's Germany sets store by the place to which she is entitled among European nations, she cannot and must not whitewash her past.

January 22, 1987

DEFIANCE IN THE GHETTO
. . .

Today's Warsaw will not reveal to the hasty visitor the profound unease that erodes the country. It is a modern city, made cheerful by greenery, with decorous, functional houses, clean and orderly, with beautiful avenues traveled by efficient public transport and few automobiles (actually, many of its citizens envy the chaotic traffic of our cities).

But it is an artificial city. The Warsaw of the thirties was almost totally destroyed—by the barbaric aerial bombings with which the Germans began invading the country without warning in 1939, and later, to a frightful extent, during the course of the national insurrection of August 1944. The torn urban fabric was reconstructed after the peace with the financial help of the Soviets, who nevertheless, having halted on the other bank of the Vistula, had left to the Germans the dirty task of liquidating the Polish national armies, for whom they themselves had little liking.

In this new city there is a singular site. In the Muranow quarter, in a modest clearing and against the anonymous background of people's housing, rises the monument to the heroes of the Ghetto: a truncated pyramid adorned with rather naïve and rhetorical high relief; but rhetoric is an integral part of monuments, and no monument exists which does not appear rhetorical after one or two generations.

But the visitor's state of mind changes abruptly when he meditates upon the events commemorated by this monument. In this city destroyed several times, Muranow was more than destroyed: it was literally razed to the ground, transformed into a desert of shattered stones, rubble, and bricks.

Against this quarter was unleashed the Germanic genius for destruction, because that was the site of the Ghetto, and because there, exactly forty years ago, took place an event that would have astonished the world, if the world had known about it. In April 1943, on the first day of Passover, a nucleus of Jews immured in the Ghetto declared war on powerful Germany, rose up in arms, incredibly won the first battle, and finally were exterminated.

In the mosaic of European resistance, the struggle of the Warsaw Ghetto occupies a unique place. Those insurgents had no rear lines at their back, they did not expect help from land or sky, they had no allies: on the contrary, for years they had been living under the most wretched conditions. All the Polish Christians had been forced to leave the restricted area of the Ghetto, which was encircled by a high wall; in their place had been settled first Warsaw's one hundred forty thousand Jews and then, gradually, other Jews coming from other cities; in January 1941 the area of the Ghetto had been further reduced, while the number of inhabitants surpassed half a million.

The crowding was frightful: from seven persons to a room it rose to ten, then actually to fifteen. The streets were permanently swarming with a desperate, restless, but above all famished crowd: food rations were less than half the vital minimum, even lower than in the *Lager*. Anyone who went beyond the wall was shot, but many, in particular the children, risked death every day to smuggle into the Ghetto food bought on the black market in the Christian city.

And yet in this citadel—polluted by the stench of the corpses that every morning lay in the streets by the hundreds, infested by rats and epidemics, terrified by the incursions of the SS—schools, libraries, synagogues, infirmaries, and associations of mutual aid functioned. So, even, did factories, whose products were destined for the German armed forces: the workers, men and women, were forced to maintain exhausting schedules for ridiculous pay, but the jobs were nevertheless sought because work was the only way to protect oneself (temporarily!) from deportation "to the East."

The notices posted on street corners spoke of agricultural labor camps, but it soon became known that they were *Lager* for total extermination, Treblinka and Belzec. But there also functioned, despite the German inspections, reprisals, and spies, the embryo of a military structure, composed almost entirely of young Zionists. Their combat experience was almost nil, and their weaponry laughable: a few pistols, rifles, and tommy-guns, in part obtained from the organization of the Polish underground, in part bought at usurious prices on the black market, in part seized from the Germans by daring raids, in part manufactured piece by piece with savage patience in the barracks-workshops that worked for the Germans.

They lacked, above all, what gave strength to the other resistances: the well-founded hope of overwhelming the enemy and surviving, if not all at least some, to build a better world. But the defenders of the Ghetto had no possibility of saving themselves, and they knew it: they could only choose between two ways of dying.

On April 18, 1943, it was learned that the Germans were preparing a mass deportation. The following day, about a thousand SS men who had entered the Ghetto were received by rifle fire and incendiary bottles flung at them, and they pulled back in disarray. The German commander was immediately replaced, and it is precisely from the reports of his successor, General Stroop, that one can measure the moral inequality between the contenders: each line he wrote gives off his *a priori* contempt for the Jews' desperate heroism.

That these Jews should know how to fight, and under such conditions, goes beyond the mental ability of Stroop, for whom his adversaries are nothing but "murderers and bandits." Without a shudder of shame, in his bureaucrat's prose, Stroop describes the Jews who throw themselves from balconies rather than surrender, the women who "shot pistols with both hands": he could not understand that whereas his men fought by blindly obeying received orders, every one of his adversaries had made a superhuman individual choice.

The unequal combat lasted for more than a month, to the ever-renewed astonishment of the Germans and the boundless rage of Hitler and Goebbels. On May 16, Stroop declares that the "great operation" is ended: but in reality, hidden among the ruins, entrenched in the network of sewers, in cellars and attics, about a hundred Jews went on fighting sporadically until December. Very few of the defenders of the Ghetto saved themselves by joining partisan groups.

At a distance of forty years and in an ever more restless world, we do not want the sacrifice of the Warsaw Ghetto insurgents to be forgotten. They have demonstrated that even when everything is lost, it is granted to man to save, together with his own dignity, that of future generations.

April 17, 1983

H A T C H I N G   T H E   C O B R A
■ ■ ■

"Let no one praise Perillus, crueler than the tyrant Phalaris, for whom he built a bull, promising him that a man locked inside it would bellow when a fire was lit beneath it, and who was the first to test on himself this torture as the fruit of a cruelty more just than his. To such an extent had he distorted a most noble art, destined to represent gods and men. Thus many of his workers had labored only to build an instrument of torture! Actually, his works are preserved for only one reason: so that whoever sees them will hate the hands of their creators." (Pliny, *Natural History*, 37.89)

There must certainly exist translations that are better than mine, but I do have a deep personal bond with old Pliny, and it seemed to me that by translating him I would pay him homage. The event is semilegendary: Pindar, Ovid, and Orosius have mentioned it, and in their footsteps so did Dante in Canto 27 of the *Inferno*. Phalaris had been the tyrant of Agrigento toward the middle of the sixth century B.C. Pliny's "whoever sees them" seems to hint at the fact that the bull, carried away by the Carthaginians in 403, had been brought back to Agrigento after the destruction of

Carthage and probably was still there during his time. Nothing is known about the reasons that moved Phalaris to burn Perillus inside his own bull.

This story, whether true or false, has a curious up-to-date flavor. For the purposes of a posthumous trial of the tyrant and his craftsmen, it would be essential to establish to which of the two should be attributed the initiative and idea for the horrendous machine. If it had been invented by Pirillus and proposed to Phalaris, there is no doubt that Pirillus, who at that time was already famous, deserved to be punished (but not necessarily in this way and by Phalaris, who by accepting the artifact had become the inventor's accomplice). He had truly, as Pliny mentions, prostituted his art and himself. He must definitely have had *un esprit mal tourné*: it must not have been easy to give the air passages of the simulacrum the correct dimensions so that the victim's moans would issue from the bronze maw amplified and modified in their harmonies, to the point of reproducing the bellowing of a bull.

If, on the other hand, Phalaris had commissioned the work, the eye-for-an-eye punishment adopted by him seems excessive and abusive: however, he was a professional tyrant, and his actions make us indignant but do not surprise us. All tyrants are capricious. By this hypothesis, Pirillus does not come out of this absolved, yet we can grant him some extenuating circumstances: perhaps he had been forced, or flattered, or threatened, or blackmailed. We don't know; but his figure as an inventor suggests modern figures and events.

Not uncommon today is the figure of the scientist who is asked to give his work for the defense of his country, or to attack a neighboring country. Everybody knows at least something about the portentous collection of brains that during the Second World War gave birth to the atomic bomb in the nick of time and to nuclear energy for peacetime use.

Some of these scientists lent their services more or less convinced, more or less gladly; others, after Hiroshima, have withdrawn to private life; still others, like Pontecorvo, have switched camps for ideological reasons, or perhaps because they thought that the nuclear weapon would be less dangerous if divided between the two superpowers.

Happily common today is the figure of the scientist who, after serving power, repents. We read not too long ago that Peter Hagelstein, a pupil of bellicose Teller, the exceedingly young "father" of the stellar shield, and a Nobel Prize candidate for physics, has left a laboratory financed by the U.S. Department of War, and has transferred to MIT, where he will work exclusively on research concerning the medical applications of the laser beam. It seems to me that there is little to object to in this sort of conscientious objection: if all the world's scientists were to imitate Hagelstein, the manufacturers of new weapons would go empty-handed and universal peace would be closer than it now appears.

I am less convinced by the position taken by Martin Ryle. Ryle, born in England in 1918, had been one of the outstanding radar specialists during the war and had contributed in a decisive manner to the measures adopted by the English to "confuse" the German radar. After the war, nauseated by the horrors of war itself, he decided to continue his brilliant career as a physicist in the field that least lent itself to belligerent applications, that is, the field of radio astronomy. He received the Nobel Prize in 1974; but he must have realized quite soon that not even his colleagues in astronomy had perfectly clean hands. For instance, to measure with precision the intensity of the gravitational field surrounding the Earth is doubtless of theoretical interest, but it also serves to improve the aim of intercontinental ballistic missiles. According to Ryle's data, 40 percent of all

English engineers and physicists are involved in the study of instruments of destruction.

Shortly before his death, which occurred in 1948, he therefore formulated a drastic proposal: "Stop science now," let us stop all scientific research, even the research that is called "basic." Since we are not in a position to foresee how any particular discovery can be distorted and exploited, let us stop: no more discoveries.

I understand the spiritual torment from which this appeal sprang, but it seems to me at once extremist and utopian. We are what we are: each one of us, even the peasant, even the most modest artisan, is a researcher, has always been that. From the undeniable danger intrinsic in each new scientific discovery we can and must protect ourselves in other ways. It is certainly true that, as Ryle says, our intelligence has increased portentously, yet our wisdom hasn't; but I ask myself how much time, in all the schools of all countries, is devoted to increasing wisdom, that is, to moral problems?

It would please me (and it seems to me neither impossible nor absurd) if in all scientific departments one point were insisted on uncompromisingly: what you will do when you exercise your profession can be useful, neutral, or harmful to mankind. Do not fall in love with suspect problems. Within the limits that you will be granted, try to know the end to which your work is directed. We know the world is not black and white and your decision may be probabilistic and difficult: but you will agree to study a new medicament, you will refuse to formulate a nerve gas.

Whether you are a believer or not, whether a "patriot" or not, if you are given a choice do not let yourself be seduced by material or intellectual interests, but choose from the field that which may render less painful and less dangerous the journey of your contemporaries, and of those who come after you. Don't hide behind the hypocrisy of neutral science: you are educated enough to be able to evaluate whether from the egg you are hatching will issue a dove or a cobra or a chimera or perhaps nothing at all. As for basic research, it can and must continue: if we were to abandon it, we would betray our nature and our nobility as "thinking reeds," and the human species would no longer have any reason to exist.

September 21, 1986

ABOUT THE AUTHOR

Primo Levi was born in Turin, Italy, in 1919, and was trained as a chemist. Arrested as a member of the anti-Fascist resistance, he was deported to Auschwitz in 1944. Levi's experience in the death camp and his subsequent travels through Eastern Europe were the subjects of his two classic memoirs, *Survival in Auschwitz* and *The Reawakening*, as well as a collection of portraits, *Moments of Reprieve*. Dr. Levi retired from his position as manager of a Turin chemical factory in 1977 to devote himself full-time to writing.

His universally acclaimed books remain a testament to the indomitability of the human spirit. He was the author of *The Periodic Table, If Not Now, When?* and *The Drowned and the Saved. The Mirror Maker* is a collection of stories and essays written for the Italian newspaper *La Stampa* and published in 1986 under the title *Racconti e saggi*. He died in Turin in April 1987.

ABOUT THE TRANSLATOR

Raymond Rosenthal is a translator and critic who has been nominated for two National Book Awards for his translations. He received the Present Tense award for his translation of Primo Levi's *The Periodic Table*. He has brought into English such famous Italian classics as Giovanni Verga's *The House by the Medlar Tree* and Pietro Aretino's *Dialogues*. He also translated *Other People's Trades* by Primo Levi.